MY PRIVILEGE, MY RESPONSIBILITY

Sheila North

A MEMOIR

GREAT PLAINS
PUBLICATIONS

Great Plains Publications
320 Rosedale Avenue
Winnipeg, MB R3L 1L8
www.greatplains.mb.ca

Great Plains Publications gratefully acknowledges the financial support provided for its publishing program by the Government of Canada through the Canada Book Fund; the Canada Council for the Arts; the Province of Manitoba through the Book Publishing Tax Credit and the Book Publisher Marketing Assistance Program; and the Manitoba Arts Council.

Design & Typography by Relish New Brand Experience
Printed in Canada by Friesens

LIBRARY AND ARCHIVES CANADA CATALOGUING IN PUBLICATION

Title: My privilege, my responsibility : a memoir / Sheila North.
Names: North, Sheila, author.
Identifiers: Canadiana (print) 20210260076 | Canadiana (ebook) 20210260157 |
   ISBN 9781773370668 (softcover) | ISBN 9781773370675 (ebook)
Subjects: LCSH: North, Sheila. | LCSH: Indigenous women—Manitoba—Biography. |
   CSH: Indigenous leaders—Manitoba—Biography. | CSH: Indigenous activists—
   Manitoba—Biography. | LCGFT: Autobiographies.
Classification: LCC E99.C88 N67 2021 | DDC 305.48/89732307127092—dc23

ENVIRONMENTAL BENEFITS STATEMENT

Great Plains Publications saved the following resources by printing the pages of this book on chlorine free paper made with 100% post-consumer waste.

TREES	WATER	ENERGY	SOLID WASTE	GREENHOUSE GASES
21	1,700	9	67	8,980
FULLY GROWN	GALLONS	MILLION BTUs	POUNDS	POUNDS

Environmental impact estimates were made using the Environmental Paper Network Paper Calculator 4.0. For more information visit www.papercalculator.org

Canadä

FSC
www.fsc.org
MIX
Paper from
responsible sources
FSC® C016245

Don't consider it a privilege or a compliment you're being asked to run, it's your responsibility.
—MARILYN WOOD

Contents

FIRST FEMALE GRAND CHIEF OF NORTHERN MANITOBA

"The results are as follows," said Stephanie Connors, the electoral officer overseeing the 2015 Manitoba Keewatinowi Okimakanak (MKO) election for Grand Chief. After a deep breath, she continued, "William 'Elvis' Thomas, 58. Sheila North Wilson, 74!" I, my campaign team, and the supporters sitting behind us in a hockey arena set up as a conference room on a sunny autumn day at the Nisichawayasihk Cree Nation (NCN) in northern Manitoba, erupted into cheers of jubilation. I took a huge sigh of relief. The election to become the first female MKO Grand Chief was the biggest race or competition of any kind that I've ever ran in and won. The echoes from our cheers reverberated back and forth in that massive space, just like in a real hockey game where the underdogs won!

I had to take a quick pause, covered my face with my hands, and took a deep breath before getting up from my seat to where my team was jumping up and down all around me. I just wanted to take it all in, this feeling of relief and joy, because the election was no easy feat. Just moments before the results were announced, the only other candidate left on the ballot had knelt down in front of me, put his right hand on my left shoulder and looked deeply into my eyes. "You did a great job Sheila, you should be proud," Elvis said. "After this I would like you to come work for me. Would you?" I didn't answer him, I was trying to stay positive for my team and my family. The other two candidates on the first ballot had been men also: the incumbent MKO Grand Chief and a young man destined for leadership. Both made a deal with Elvis and all three got together for the second and final ballot to try and win the seat for Elvis Thomas. They made sure all of the 150 or so delegates who make up part of northern Manitoba Chiefs, Councils and citizens, knew what they were up to.

This was my first time running in an election, besides running for a student council seat years before at a college in Brandon. But no one else had run at that time so I got in by acclamation! But the MKO election would not be my last. Three years later, in July 2018, I ran for the position of the Assembly of First Nations National Chief. I came in second, in the second ballot. In both elections, men were very prominent and their needs and wants were well represented. Women also made their voices heard but their messages were different from the men. In general, both wanted the best for their communities, families, and themselves, but generally, the men I came across wanted to win at any cost. So much so, they worked together to stand up against me as a challenger and worked to intimidate me. I was in an abusive relationship for eight years, so I knew these types of tactics very well. But I also know most of that behaviour stems from colonization, when our matriarchal societies were thrown into chaos by settler men who insisted on talking with our patriarchs only. The actions and decisions from that time still have their effects on all of us today. More on that later!

During this leg of my lifelong journey though, we had just won a hard-fought battle that actually began many generations before. MKO was set up to represent the northern region of Manitoba and its thirty communities of Cree, Dene, and Oji-Cree peoples—a population of about 72,000 plus people. MKO was created in 1981 by Chiefs and other leaders to advocate for Northerners and their needs. The founders wanted to make sure the needs of the region and its people were met and respected. Unfortunately, the region was and still is one of the poorest regions in Canada. It has a high poverty rate, lack of sufficient and proper housing and infrastructure, and some of the highest numbers of illnesses such as diabetes, cancer, and tuberculosis.

The challenges are great in the region, but there are things that people celebrate like the high numbers of people who still speak their languages, that they've managed to keep many traditional hunting and fishing grounds intact, and that most First Nations from the North still call their home reserves home. Up to seventy percent of northerners still live in their home reserves.

On the day of the MKO election at the Nisichawayasihk Cree Nation it was a perfect fall day. The sun was shining, no wind, no clouds, it was warm. Perfect. We had gathered over three days listening to the leaders at the tables talking and debating about issues that affect our people, lands, and water in the North. And on that beautiful day in September 2015, the Chiefs, Councillors, and proxies voted in the first female Grand Chief in its over thirty years of existence. The win was bigger than myself and my team.

As my team and I drove into the Cree community on election day, three eagles flew overhead as if they were leading us into town where there was a sacred fire lit in a tipi next to the arena. It was hard to miss the majestic eagles circling close by. As we parked, we stood there for a minute admiring them circling overhead with the smell from the sacred fire wafting in air. A Fire Keeper, who was likely there all night, spoke up and told us he had noticed the majestic birds flying near the site since the meetings started the day before. He would definitely notice; he and other Fire Keepers would take turns making sure the fire lit at the beginning of the leaders' conference would stay lit until the end of the gathering. Elders have said seeing eagles at any time, especially in situations you least expect to see them, is a good sign. It could mean Creator is reminding you that any messages or prayers are being heard, or it could mean for the person who sees an eagle to be careful. To be mindful. So, it was an encouraging sign, an uplifting sign, to see the birds and the Fire Keeper recognized the significance as well. To me, seeing the eagles that day was a reminder from Creator that all is well, and he is in control no matter what. That moment was an end to a busy but short campaign, about five weeks in total. Two of my team members and I tucked into the tipi next to the sacred fire before going inside in the arena for the meeting. Tobacco in hand, we held hands, I prayed a short prayer and we all cried quietly. I think we were feeling a sense of completion and felt accomplished no matter what the outcome would be.

As I finished praying, I wiped my tears and said, "No more tears, time to finish the work." We had a little laugh and headed inside. My first intention was to straighten my hair in the bathroom! We had a late night and early morning, so I didn't have time to get fully ready before we left our hotel rooms in Thompson, Manitoba that morning. Thompson, one of the main urban centres in northern Manitoba, is about an hour's drive from NCN. It's where most of us delegates stayed during the assembly.

That morning, I was invited to have breakfast with one community's Chief and Councillors before heading to the voting site. We had a great discussion, and I was feeling inspired knowing I was able to relate quickly to the needs of their community. I was able to relate because I grew up in the North, in Bunibonibee Cree Nation, and I had worked as a journalist for ten years leading up to the election. I know the issues and hardships very well.

As my campaign manager and longtime friend, Jennifer Wood, and I stood in the bathroom waiting for our hair straighteners to heat up, her husband, my friend Darcy Wood, frantically came to the door of the bathroom and yelled our names, almost as if he was warning us about a fire or some other emergency. It was a bit of an emergency: there was a change in plans none of us anticipated. He wanted us to come out quickly because it was announced that the final candidate speeches were starting, and my name was the first one called.

This was not the initial plan. The night before, the organizers told us that the speeches would start at noon and the order of appearance for final speeches would be by a random draw. We arrived at the site at ten a.m. and thought we had a couple of hours to review my ten-minute speech again and finish getting ready. But no, it was time to go. As I walked out of the bathroom, one of my other team members, Clyde Flett, quickly walked up to me saying the audio-visual equipment was not set up. Just the day before a large 10 x 10-foot screen was set up right next to the Chiefs table where presenters were able to pull up PowerPoints as they talked. My team and I had spent a lot of time working on my PowerPoint presentation. My final speech was timed out perfectly with the visuals, and Clyde had the thumb drive ready to plug in to the system. He'd tested it the day before and it worked beautifully. But on this day, as we walked into the conference area, the screen was gone and so was the projector that used to sit on the table next to the head table. It's almost as if the equipment had never been there.

When I came out of the bathroom with all my things and my notebook with my perfectly crafted speech, Clyde met me at the door. With the thumb drive in his hand he said, "we won't have PowerPoint." I said, "What?" in disbelief. Clyde was shocked as well. He played a big part in our preparation, and he was equally invested in our campaign. He would have been the one next to me helping me deliver my speech by operating the PowerPoint we had worked on so meticulously. I was disappointed of course, but I knew we had to keep going. I just said, "Okay!" It was almost like when you jump into some cold water after being hot all day. I felt shocked and at the same time, exhilarated as I walked toward the head table to make my way to the podium. I felt like I was walking fast and determined. The movie *Forrest Gump* came to mind, that one scene where Gump's leg braces were falling off as he began to run!

As I finally got up to the podium, I looked around and saw all the faces, hundreds of them. More had come to observe the voting process. Chiefs, Councillors, and spectators ready to listen to what the four candidates had to say. We each had ten minutes and there was a large digital timer in front of the podium, blinking, waiting, taunting. No one said go, or even gave a warning of a start time, there was no countdown, the clock just started counting down as I stepped in front of the mantel. My younger brother Steven and an Elder from my home community slowly got up and came to stand next to me as I began my speech. I was reminded of a story that the Elder, Dorothy Grieves, told me the day before about how my late dad had recruited her and helped her run for Chief of our community when she was a young woman. Dorothy said, "Your dad helped me when I became Chief of our community. He said he was looking for a replacement. That he had other plans for his family and that I would be the best suited for the community. I'm so grateful your dad helped me and want to stand with you for your dad and your mom."

I felt honoured that she stood there with my brother and me because she was a trailblazer for our people. She gave me a big, beautiful smile as she was done telling the story. She is a respected Elder in our North and is one of the Elders who is always invited to sit in on Chiefs' meetings.

She was comfortable doing that and people love her. Dorothy also makes some of the best beadwork and handcrafts like moccasin slippers. Anyone who's ever been gifted her slippers would be so happy with her skills. I have two pairs of her work, one pair of slippers I haven't worn yet. I want to keep them in mint condition. I wanted her to know I valued her presence and stories.

My brother being there with me made me feel the strength of my parents and family who couldn't make the trip to the election. Steven was the only one there with me from my immediate family. Our family is very close, and we all communicate often. Him being there was an extension of our whole family. With him there, it felt like they were all there: my mom, my dad, my children, my siblings, and other relatives. "I woke up that morning and Dad called me and asked me to go to the election," Steven said. "So, I came even though I had worked a night shift just hours before." I appreciated his decision very much. So did our parents.

The speech I gave was perfectly crafted with four main points. It was so well designed I could still recite it on cue if I have to! The four main points we called Cornerstones were, 1. Accountable and Transparent Governance, 2. Empowering Communities and Families, 3. Meaningful Treaty Implementation, and 4. Economic Independence. In short, the speech was geared toward seeking out and supporting the vision of the leaders and people of MKO, the past and current aspirations. I was most proud of the fact that we recognized the sovereignty of the Nations and we wanted to honour that. I still do.

After speaking to leaders and experts about Indigenous politics and knowing what I knew from my work as a journalist, my team and I worked hard to narrow down the main points I wanted to include in my platform. A friend and mentor, Barbara Bowes, who coaches people and organizations for success, helped us with the structure of the speech. It became easy to recite, especially because one of my campaign managers, Darcy, reminded me about ten times a day to practice my speech. He'd call me, text me, and every time I saw him, he'd simply ask, "Did you do your speech?" Most of the time I'd say yes before he would ask me, even if I hadn't. But he reminded me so often that toward the end of the campaign I was reciting the speech at least four times a day randomly as I worked, worked out, or drove in my vehicle. I did as much as I could throughout the days leading up to the election. Thank goodness for all that, because being caught off-guard just minutes before could have thrown me off if we hadn't been as prepared as we were. I was able to deliver the speech in the time allotted and used every second of it and not one second more. I felt really good about it. Being trained and having been a journalist certainly helped with the smooth delivery as well.

In some elections for Grand Chief, it's only Chiefs who get to vote. For MKO, the Council members also get to vote, so we had a larger than usual voter base—and we had more people to appeal to. This election went to two ballots, the rules are that the ballots keep going until one candidate has 51 percent of the vote, and that candidate wins the election. I was leading in the first ballot. In between the first and second ballot we all had chances to caucus again and meet community leaders who started grouping together to wait for us candidates to come to them. This is when the three other candidates declared they were going to join forces and support Elvis Thomas, who had come in second in the first ballot. Turns out, as Indigenous politics would have it, Elvis and I were long-lost cousins on our fathers' sides. He told me this during the campaign, in between other comments he made mostly about me being a woman. Saying things like, "good for you for trying, that's so nice," and almost patting me on the head a few times when we met on the campaign trail.

Soon, as the electoral officer announced the timing of the next round of results for the next ballot, tension filled the room. At least it did for me. I remember feeling a sense of panic as the room seemed to grow larger and hollower than before. I turned to Jennifer, who has and had been one of my biggest supporters and motivators, and asked her, "what do we do now?" Without a flinch she said, "Let's go." As we made our way around the room there were several circles of Chiefs and Councillors grouping together. The first group we approached said, "Don't worry about us, we're with you. Go talk to Island Lake."

Island Lake was made up of four Oji-Cree communities, who refer to themselves in their own language as Anishiniwuk—The People. The large group of about thirty or so were gathered outside the arena in a closed circle huddled together. It was hard to find a spot to go in from, but Darcy said, "Just go in there." I did, and all of a sudden, I was standing in the middle of the circle. Immediately they stopped talking as I stood there not knowing at first what to say or even where to look. I felt the world was suddenly quiet and it was watching me as I started to feel I was leaving my body. But reality hit me pretty quickly as I started to speak. I remember saying something like, "I know your people are unique and have your own culture and language, I respect that." I also added that one of their own people, the late and great Elijah Harper, "was and still is one of my mentors and heroes and I respect where he comes from." I told the tightknit group around me that my late father and Elijah had been friends for many years and were former fellow leaders themselves. I wanted them to know that I was very familiar with one of their most respected and loved leaders. And of course, it wasn't just me. Elijah Harper became a hero to many of us for infamously saying 'No' to the Meech Lake Accord in 1990 as a Member of the Legislative Assembly with the Manitoba provincial government. At the time Elijah was representing the same region MKO covered and to many of us he was saying NO to Canada walking over us to give a group of Canadians greater status than its Original People, us.

After talking in the circle of Anishiniwuk, we talked to a few more groups and then I was called to go back in the Island Lake huddle. Again, it was very intense and all I could do was again reinforce what I had said just moments earlier. Shortly after that, the delegates started lining up again to cast their ballots. I happened to be standing where the lineup was forming, and I had a chance to greet and shake the hands of everyone lining up to vote. I thanked them for their consideration in voting for me. As I was shaking the hand of one Council member, she left something in my hand. She leaned in and said, "don't worry." I looked at what she had placed in my hand, and I felt a sense of calm. It was a smooth stone that had the word "HOPE" on it. I needed that and I realized we had done all we could.

As we found our way back to our seats, we sat quietly and only whispered when we talked. In fact, the room was also very silent; you could almost hear a pin drop at times. I looked behind me once to see some of my relatives from my dad's side and original home reserve, Pimicikamak Cree Nation, who'd travelled in that day to be with us. But I didn't want to look too long at them otherwise I'd get emotional. I missed my kids, my parents, my siblings, but I felt they were all there knowing my brother was there with me. My husband, Rob, was there too, but he didn't say much. It was almost as if he wasn't even there at times. Which suited me fine because I didn't have the time or mindset during those moments to make sure he was okay or comfortable. Not as much as I normally would, though I appreciated him being there.

Once I was declared the winner and we stopped jumping up and down in celebration, the official inauguration started. I could see Elvis, who came in second, crouching and covering his face too after the results were announced. Then all of a sudden, he was right next to me. "Congratulations Sheila," he simply said. And it felt like he wanted to say more, but I was distracted by the fact that my husband was waiting to hug me and congratulate me. "Thank you, Elvis," I said and almost literally had to push past him so I could hug my family and friends who were waiting to greet me. I didn't want to be rude, but I was wondering why he was lingering on. I really don't know what he was feeling, but I suspect it wasn't a good feeling for him. Moments before the announcement, the scrutineer for Elvis's campaign, who was standing next to my brother who was my scrutineer, against a wall to the right of us, was snickering. From that and my brother's poker face, I was sure we had lost but was pleasantly surprised when the outcome was finally announced. I'm still confused as to why Elvis's scrutineer was giggling so much; my brother said he didn't understand that either.

After the announcement, a Pipe Ceremony was set up quickly with songs shared as I was being prepped by host Elders and their helpers to declare the Oath of Office. The Elders told me that there would be a Pipe Ceremony to officially recognize the results of the election and me as the new Grand Chief in a Cree traditional way. "I have to tell you I'm on my time though," I said to Elder David Sanderson, meaning my period that started that morning. "It's okay," he said. "Just cover yourself and don't touch the pipe for now. I'll help you, don't worry." A Pipe Ceremony is very important for official occasions like this and signifies that some important decisions have been made. Using the pipe invokes our wishes to Creator that we are seeking a blessing for the decisions made. Women or girls on their periods are not allowed to participate in the passing of the pipe because they are too powerful during this time. If anyone on their period participates in ceremonies, they could pull all the energy away from the intent of the ceremony and could cause harm. I learned a bit more about this teaching as I started working as a Grand Chief. I will elaborate further on what I learned later. I will say for now, I appreciate my 'moon' time and I don't think of it as inconvenient anymore!

After the ceremony, I was back at the podium prepped to read out loud the MKO Oath of Office. In it I declared to uphold the MKO Constitution and respect all people in the region: men, women, boys, and girls. It was extremely empowering and exciting to be there. I will never forget the faces I saw and the feelings I felt as I read the Oath. It almost felt like I was standing on water or up high with wind blowing by. Even though being a leader wasn't a dream I'd always had for myself, standing there that day was a surreal experience.

The next day, when it was all said and done, we had a quick meeting with nervous MKO staff and I joked to ease the tension and asked with my hand out, "Can I have the keys to my helicopter now?" We all laughed! Our people have been using humour for many generations to get over all kinds of stressful or even painful situations. Truthfully though, I was just as nervous as they were. I had never been a manager or leader of a group this size before, let alone the group of Chiefs and Councillors who voted me in. It was a daunting task to think about, but I felt ready to take it on.

When we were done and leaving the arena for the day, I looked to Jennifer walking beside me and said, "Let's go, this is all your doing!" We laughed some more, but I meant it with her. In a good but also joking way. She and Darcy made the win possible. So, with a big sigh and a good laugh, I started my three-year term as the first female Grand Chief of the Manitoba Keewatinowi Okimakanak.

Chapter 2

IS SHE A QUEEN?

As a child, I thought we were rich. I thought we lived in the best house, had the best life, had the best clothes, and had the best parents. I felt blessed beyond belief. My positive childhood experiences are what I attribute my ideas of 'privilege' to, not knowing then that the reality was much different from what I knew as a child. The isolated community I grew up in was and still is one of the poorest communities in our country. Most homes didn't have running water or sewer lines. Our house had some running water, but we had to fill the tank ourselves with water from the lake during all four seasons until the community started a water delivery service. We had some sewer lines but most of the time they didn't work, so part of my and my siblings' chores were to fill the water tanks and empty the 'slop pails' where we would go pee or poop! Sometimes, when the pail was too full, the contents of it would spill on the side of our leg that the pail was on. Still, doing that chore was just part of our lives, nothing out of the ordinary then. Today, some homes still don't have running water or sewer lines. So, some still live this way on reserves, especially in isolated communities.

When I was born, my parents, Gilbert and Sadie (Weenusk) North, and my two older siblings, who were just toddlers at the time, were living in a small trailer in my mom's community called Oxford House, now known by its Cree name, Bunibonibee Cree Nation. Bunibonibee means 'the place where there is a very deep hole in the lake.' My eldest living relative says there used to be mermaids in the lake, or as she called them 'kinosih iskwewuk.'

Visitors to Bunibonibee often say they feel something special about our community after they meet people and see the lake that surrounds our community. It's a beautiful deep lake. As a child I woke up every morning seeing the lake as our house, like most houses on reserve, was nestled right along its shore.

One of our Elders, Jack Grieves, tells me the lake is very deep in places and has subterranean tunnels. "The tunnels came from deep holes made by sturgeon fish," said Jack. "The tunnels lead from one spot in a lake to another." Our community now sits approximately 925 kilometers northeast of Winnipeg, but it wasn't the original place our people and ancestors lived. There were a few settlements near where our reserve is now, but people were forced to settle in one area during Treaty negotiation time.

"Before we settled here," Jack said, "we were nomadic. We moved around all over the North and had several forts set up. Our people, like other Indigenous people, even lived down south and moved back up North when they needed to. There are many people who live down in southern Manitoba and other provinces that used to live up North too, including Chief Peguis and Sioux Indians" he added. "We all followed the moose, wild game, and a variety of fish before everyone settled in different areas during the fur trade." Jack also says we had our own political systems as different tribes and we as Cree had our own alliance when we dealt with other tribes. He says our people were independent, strong, and self-sufficient.

In 1972, when I was born, our community was fully settled in. Right in the middle of the reserve next to a former school site was a small blue and white trailer where my parents lived with my two older sisters. My mom says the trailer was home to teachers before and it was very drafty. When I was teething, my mom got worried that the trailer was too cold for me to be in. Mom still has pictures of the little trailer, to me it looks more like a smaller RV. It was a good temporary home for my parents with their growing family though, before that they lived with my mom's parents and siblings, about nine people in a small three-bedroom house. My dad set out to find another place to live when the Chief, Dorothy Grieves, the same Elder who came to stand with me during the MKO election, offered to have us stay in one of the most modern houses in the community where a school principal used to live. It had a million-dollar view overlooking the very clear and clean lake that you can still drink water from today. The house was sitting empty at the time, so we moved into the three-bedroom house with a basement, running water and a flushable toilet and working tub. This type of house was and still is very rare in most isolated communities, so you see where some of the feeling of 'privilege' comes from. But the plumbing system didn't always work, and the basement wasn't livable, so my five siblings and I had to share two of the available bedrooms. Still, I am grateful we had the old house. It's where I lived my whole life until I moved away as a fifteen-year-old to go to high school in Winnipeg.

I am the middle child in our family. I have two older sisters, Audrey and Kathleen. Rachel and Steven are both younger than me, as is our adopted brother, Harry. We grew up going to church every Wednesday, Friday, and twice on Sundays. It was just a matter of life for us, and I now see how much this part of our childhood taught us. It taught me self-discipline and how to listen to other people speaking for long periods of time!

As I got older, school became more important to me every year. I never had a choice to go to school or not, I had to go. And I had to do well or at least always try to do well. Achieving and progressing in school, and eventually every other opportunity since my childhood, is always something I had to do. I felt I had no choice, but I'm glad. I appreciate my parents for teaching me to be a high achiever. The work ethic has carried me throughout every role and situation I've found myself in since. Even though I didn't always win, I was taught to do my best with honesty, integrity, and honour.

My parents made sure my siblings and I did well in school. They wouldn't let us skip classes for any reason unless we were very ill. They also wouldn't let us get in any kind of trouble at school and year after year, I and my siblings would get perfect attendance awards. At the time, a disciplined childhood was normal to me even though I did not always like it. I wanted to be free the way I saw my friends to be, so I thought. Through it all though, and as I became a parent and adult myself, I appreciate the self-discipline my parents instilled in me. I appreciate the way they taught me to work hard and make the most of what I had.

I loved learning and getting good marks. I can still recall some of the names of my teachers and have a memory of each grade. Not to say I don't have bad memories from that time, but the good memories are stronger. One of the best ones is being in grade 5. I had a teacher named Mr. Patzer. It seemed like a normal day that day, until someone came to our classroom and asked for me. Mr. Patzer released me, and I was taken to the main office. My dad was waiting for me there, looking happy. He took my hand and said we had to go home and change for a special occasion, but he didn't say what the event was for. Didn't matter, I was happy to see him and have him take me out of school in the middle of the day. It was very exciting because I rarely got to miss school. We went home and Mom had me put on a frilly white dress shirt and curled my bangs. All I knew at this point was our school was getting some special visitors.

When we got back to the school, the gym was set up for an assembly and there were visitors standing around. RCMP officers with their red serge uniforms, men dressed in suits, including Mr. Patzer who didn't usually wear a suit. And then there was this really beautiful and tall blonde woman wearing a red dress suit in the middle of it all. She was certainly noticeable and immediately I knew she was someone important. "Is she a Queen," I wondered! Turns out, she was Pearl McGonigal, the first woman to hold the post of Lieutenant Governor in Manitoba and only the second female Lieutenant Governor in Canada.

The Honourable Pearl McGonigal was in Bunibonibee on official duties of course and brought an award she wanted to present to the best student in the whole school, at least that's my interpretation! And that student was me! I was introduced to her, she congratulated me for being such a good student and wished me well for the future. I stared at her beautiful almost platinum blonde hair tied up in a bun and looked into her blue eyes feeling overwhelmed and amazed to see her and everyone else in our school gym. I remember my dad beaming with pride and it made me feel proud. Back then of course, I had no idea I was looking into the eyes of the first woman Lieutenant Governor of Manitoba, and I know she didn't realize she was looking into the eyes of the future first female Grand Chief of Northern Manitoba either!

I was really happy to get the award but so were my parents and Mr. Patzer. But as soon as the presentation was done, that was it, the commotion moved somewhere else. Still, I have a plaque and picture to prove that I received the Governor General's Academic Medal in Grade 5. I will never forget that red dress suit Ms. McGonigal wore. I've wanted one like it since and sometimes I wear my hair like she did that day.

Another distinct memory I have is getting ready for a science fair in Garden Hill, one of the Oji-Cree reserves close by. We had to take a short plane ride from our community to Garden Hill and stayed overnight in the community, camping out in the school library. I'd already won the science fair at our school for a water distillation project. I was going over last-minute details about my project with my science teacher, Mr. Lindsay, before we left for the science fair. I asked him, "So when I win and the judges ask me about the uses for the water, can I say we can use it in emergencies?" Mr. Lindsay's reply was, "Oh what makes you so sure you're going to win there too?" I don't feel it was mean-spirited when he asked me, maybe he was trying to help keep my expectations low. But at that moment, I was actually questioning myself and thinking, "Do you mean I could actually lose?" I had not thought of that possibility until that moment.

I'm not sure why, maybe it was because my parents and I set high standards, but I genuinely wondered if I could actually lose. I had won every contest I had entered before that, including creative writing contests. Well, I did lose that science fair, I think because I focussed on losing rather than winning. Or someone else actually had a better science project. My next science project was an electrical board that was also a matching game. I put bodies on one side and heads on the other side and connected wires in the back with tin foil. The user would then use wires connected to a battery and a small lightbulb to figure out the matches. The right matches lit up the little bulb. It was pretty cool, I thought. But I don't remember entering another science fair after my devastating loss. I lost my mojo for it!

But I was still a great student. I took a lot of pride in always being in the top three of getting the high marks in our classes, next to my childhood best friends Beryl and Jacqueline. There were other smart kids in class of course, but we three seemed to be in competition for high marks with each other all the time, or maybe it was just me competing with them.

The other clear memory is being a little different from other students where I, along with my siblings, weren't allowed to stay at school for lunch. Partly because we lived so close to it, but mostly because my mom always had lunch for us to go home to. We weren't allowed on the school buses either for those same reasons. I realize my mom was very strict with us because she wanted the best for us, she wanted to make sure we were always safe and taken care of. That meant we were with her at home as much as we could be. As a child I don't think I always appreciated that and I likely took it for granted sometimes, but we only asked maybe once each to stay at school for lunch or take a bus to a friend's place or our grandparents' place. It was always no and that was final.

I didn't question my parents' decisions either, nor did I dare disobey. Mom was the disciplinarian in our family and if Dad had to step in to help her, then we were in real trouble. Spanking was the main form of punishment and it only had to happen a few times because Mom's messages got through. The spanking seemed harsh when it happened, but it wasn't bad enough for me to feel any negative feelings towards my parents for it. In fact, we later laughed about some of the spanking sessions we experienced. I know my parents had our best interest at heart and I appreciate the way they taught us about right and wrong.

There were very rare occasions when we were allowed to stay at school for lunch. Mostly, when my parents were out of town and we had to stay with our grandparents or other relatives. So, it was very exciting for me to stay at school for lunch even though the lunches were usually peanut butter and jam sandwiches on white bread or Klik canned meat sandwiches and watered-down Tang, powdered flavoured juice.

For people who have never had the pleasure of eating Klik, I dare you to try some. You'll find it in most grocery or convenience stores. Klik is likely the most popular or most well-known brand of canned meat, even with different brands, most people I know call those small rectangular cans of meat products with its own can opener glued to the bottom of the can, Klik.

The consistency of the meat is very mushy, salty and a blob of gelatin usually comes plopping out when you open the can and slide it onto a plate or frying pan. If you try frying the pinkish lunch meat it almost disintegrates because of the high fat content in it. You'll need to fry it at a lower temperature. I don't know what the actual nutritional value of the product is, but I do know it became a staple for many families who lived and live in First Nations communities. It usually costs less than actual cuts of pork or other meat. To me it tasted okay in between pieces of bannock, another Indigenous food staple in recent decades.

The type of food I ate as a child was much different from what my parents ate as children. In just over a decade or two, food security and insecurity became a big issue for Indigenous people in Canada. As with most things in life, when you introduce products that should make life easier or more convenient, life changes. Not always for the better. My parents and their parents ate mostly from the land: moose, sturgeon, berries. And they were healthier. I saw a video from a Treaty Day event in the '60s of people who've passed on from my community. The men and women seemed to have no problem getting up and down from sitting on the ground for example. And no one seemed to be overweight.

Just a few decades later and until now, you will find in our Indigenous communities, some of the highest rates of various illnesses in the country, largely because of food that is accessible and not accessible for many on reserves. Food items such as Klik are prime examples of the type of food that is readily available and affordable now. For many, the price of groceries and fresh produce on reserve and even in urban centres for some Indigenous people are not affordable. The levels of poverty, maintained by government policies, also hinder Indigenous people's ability to hunt and fish for better and culturally appropriate food. All of it is a recipe for disaster that contributes to high rates of diabetes, cancer, suicide, poverty, and mental illness for Indigenous people in Canada.

On the lighter side, some Indigenous comedians have labeled Klik 'comfort food.' For sure, when you visit some Elders in their homes today, you will likely be offered Red Rose tea with bannock and Klik. Red Rose tea was readily available at reserve grocery stores and for many it was the only type of tea they'd drink. Purity Pilot biscuits are another popular food item, a larger and hard type of soda biscuit that is cheaper to buy than all the ingredients needed to make bannock.

But when I think about it too long, it hurts me to know that food insecurity is literally killing the Original People of these rich lands we now call Canada. To me, Klik and other cheaper food items like it, represent a big part of the degradation of Our People!

As a child at home though, I didn't know how bad food insecurity was and was getting. For lunch break, my mom usually had warm soup and a variety of meat sandwiches with mayonnaise and tomatoes or lettuce. That's partly why I feel I had a privileged childhood, having had lunches of substance compared to the smaller lunches of other children and the types of food that was offered at school. Though sometimes I felt deprived when I wasn't allowed to stay at school with my friends for lunch, the grass did seem greener on the other side then. Sometimes.

Not all of my childhood memories are about school though. Some memories from that time are scary and unhappy. One bad memory is being swarmed by a pack of dogs. It's not just a stereotype, some of our First Nations are overrun with dogs who've become stray dogs living in the woods. That's why there are shooting days to control the populations. Stray dogs are a problem, like many things on reserves, largely due to the lack of resources to deal with the issue. Lack of resources because of the lack of funding for reserves. But ultimately, I see all of the lack of resources on reserves caused by a lack of political will by federal, provincial and municipal governments to level up resources to the real needs of their Indigenous neighbours and Treaty partners.

My scary experience with a pack was as a young child, not sure how old I was, maybe nine years old but I wasn't very tall. Not that I'm tall now, but I was a lot shorter! I remember because the large dogs, about five of them, came up to about my ribcage. I was walking home and I wasn't too far from there, when all of a sudden, the dogs literally came and surrounded me, growling with their big teeth glistening in the sun. I tried to talk to them in a friendly tone, I love dogs. I kept trying to talk to them trying not to sound panicked. I even reached my hands out to them, trying to calm them down some as they kept circling and growling, one almost whining. This went on for a few minutes, but it felt like an eternity. I've heard of other kids being mauled by dogs and one of my nephews was mauled and scarred by a dog.

Then, suddenly, one of the dogs to had mercy on me. I couldn't tell which of them were males or females, but I felt like the one who showed some compassion was a female. I reached my hand to her, and she licked my palm. She then turned around to stand next to me barking at the others to calm down! The rest of the pack did start to slow their aggression towards me until an adult came running from a house nearby and yelled to scare them off. Finally, the dogs stopped and ran off. I'll always be grateful for that one dog who showed kindness! Interestingly, the same feeling I felt being surrounded by the pack of dogs I felt again in an election I ran in years later. Except it was men who surrounded me, trying to rip me to shreds. More about that later.

Another constant negative memory is dealing with bullies. One of the things my mom and dad said in Cree every time we left the house to go to school was, 'Don't say anything back to anyone who says anything to you.' I took that to heart, and it is still unnatural to me to say anything back to anyone who says anything negative to me. I never felt comfortable in any type of confrontation, not even with bullies. Though it got easier to stand up for other people than it ever was to stand up for myself.

Most of the time I had to deal with a bully it was about growing up in a Christian home. Other kids would make fun of us for having to go to church and not being able to go to dances or other events that other kids were allowed to go to. I'm not sure why it was such a big deal that we went to church all the time, but it certainly was reason enough for other kids to make fun of us. But no matter how bad the bullying was, I was never allowed to talk back. The few times the bullying got physical, Mom and Dad would hear about it, and it was me and my siblings who'd be in trouble for it, at home. It didn't matter to me if I responded to bullies, I got in trouble either way. The good part of all that though is, I have a high tolerance for negativity and negative people. It takes a great deal for me to respond to bullies.

Chapter 3

MY PARENTS AS CHILDREN

My parents, Gilbert and Sadie, are incredible people when you consider where they've come from and what they've had to overcome. My late father, who passed away October 15, 2017, was raised by his grandparents in Pimicikamak Cree Nation also known as Cross Lake, Manitoba. Pimicikamak is another majestic northern Cree settlement. Also surrounded by water, the community has a history of troubled waters largely due to a hydro development dam, Jenpeg, near the reserve. We visited our relatives in Pimicikamak at least once a year, sometimes more than that. One distinct memory I have of one of these visits to the community was seeing no water near the shores. The hydroelectric dam had a lot of control of the water to produce electricity for the province. The community's need to hunt and fish for sustenance became secondary, to say the least, to production of electricity for the province.

The community had many other challenges but also such beauty; it shaped the values of many great leaders and people, including my late and wonderful father. My dad told us stories about living with his grandparents his sister, Theresa, and a younger brother in a small log cabin home. They lived simply and happily. His brother was a tall and extremely talented artist, who tragically died in a house fire in the 1970s. Dad eventually took care of his grandparents, Geordie and Martha North, in their elder years until he married my mom when he was twenty-eight years old.

One vivid story he told me about himself as a teenager was when he was about fifteen years old and he heard about his young mother passing away. While out on the land where he was tasked to take care of dog teams used for hunting by community members, someone showed up to tell him he had to go home to hear something about his mom. She had tuberculosis and was sent away for treatment. But neither he nor his grandparents knew where she was and how long she'd be gone. He says they were always wondering until the word came that day that she'd died. He remembered how shocking the news was for him and how much he cried for her. He told me in his later years he always cried for his mom and missed her so much. For nearly fifty years he didn't know where she ended up and what it was like for her as she passed. Our people, our family stay very close to people when they're passing, part of it I think is because they don't want people to feel alone as they pass on. It must've been hard on my dad and his grandparents to know they weren't able to be with my dad's mom, Madeline North. From stories from my dad's close cousins, it sounds like my late grandmother was a teen mom, had at least three living children before she was sent away, and was very kind.

Dad was never comfortable talking too much about his late mother. In fact, I don't remember too many stories he told about his mom, other than to say she abandoned him. He felt she abandoned him most of his life, but I think he felt that way because he lost the only parent he had at such a young age. Both of them. His father wasn't around.

Since that time though, he'd found some closure. The story he said he heard all along was that she was buried in a mass grave somewhere near a TB hospital near The Pas, Manitoba. He told us once that he went to a site where there is supposed to be a mass grave near an old hospital to pay his respects to his mother. He didn't know exactly where the gravesite was or how many people might be buried there, but he said he fell to his knees crying and praying, missing his mom.

No one had been able to tell him and the family where his mom was actually laid to rest. It wasn't until a few decades later when a volunteer researcher responding to one of my cousin's social media posts calling for help, that my kookom, my grandmother Madeline's, gravesite was located. It was far from The Pas where she was last said to be. It came as a huge surprise for all of us. Dad had struggled his whole life not knowing where his mother was. The gravesite is in Brandon, Manitoba marked with a flat stone that has my grandmother's name misspelled on it. Around her resting place are other markers labeled as 'unknown.' Who knew, all that time and when I lived in Brandon for four years that my grandmother was buried there. Thankfully, Dad was able to find out where his mother was after all those years of not knowing. He cried like a baby when he found out and actually called out, "Mommy," when he first heard about the discovery. To me he was carrying a story of an #MMIW victim. Murdered by the systems meant to help people get well. Missing from the family who loved her for five decades. Sadly, her story is not the only one about TB victims. There are many more stories yet to be told. Similar to stories now known about survivors and thrivers of the Indian Residential Schools and the Sixties Scoop and those that didn't make it home.

The day my relatives, my dad, and our family decided to visit the gravesite in Brandon, with the volunteer researcher who found the grave was a beautiful summer day in 2017, just months before my dad would pass away himself. I had to join virtually because I was at work as the MKO Grand Chief in a meeting about children in care. My dad was very emotional, and I felt so sorry that he never really got to know his mom or know where she was almost his entire life. I'm not sure why the hospital or government officials never told the family where my late grandmother's body was laid to rest or what her life was like in her last years or what the last days of her life were like for her. But it was cruel. Someone needed to tell my dad where his mom was all along. Many more families need to know where their loved ones are. And there needs to be some accountability and recognition of what happened to TB victims who died in government-run hospitals that some say were used as places to do medical experiments on our relatives.

What we do know is she had another child, a girl, who was adopted out to a non-Indigenous family in Minnedosa, Manitoba, just north of Brandon. The girl is of course a grown woman now who told me via email that she didn't want to meet us. The woman's sister reached out to us after seeing the coverage of my dad's story in the *Brandon Sun* that year. The woman told us that my dad's sister grew up being scared of Native people and that she didn't want to meet us. Apparently, she is a beautiful and caring woman who never married or had kids of her own. We'll never know, I guess. At least my late father got to see where his mother was buried. He died about six months after that. He never met his long-lost sister. My aunt Theresa, the sister my dad grew up with, was hoping to meet her before she passed, but that didn't happen either.

We did see pictures of the aunt none of my family have ever met. She sticks out very clearly among the white family who adopted her. She has a kind face and has the same beautiful dark complexion that my late dad and other North relatives have. Four years after Dad passed, one of my other cousins found a black and white photo of my late grandmother Madeline. In the photo she is petite, smiling, lying in a hospital bed. Alone. I hope somehow she knows she was loved, not only by the people she already had in her life, but those of us who came after her too.

My mother, Sadie, knew her parents very well. She was a momma's girl, very close to her mom, my late kookom Betsy Weenusk. She remembers as a young child cleaning the floors with her mom, both on hands and knees. She says my kookom would pick her up by the back of her shirt to move to another spot to clean. She must've been so tiny. She was one of ten children. Her family was very close, and her mom was the centre of her life until she met my dad as a twenty-year-old lady. She too grew up in Bunibonibee and also lived there her whole life until she was sent to residential school as a young teen far away from her family.

My mom was the third oldest of the big family, she was very devoted to her parents, Betsy and Wesley Weenusk. Mom wanted to be a nurse. The closest she came to that was being a midwife in the community. But she is a natural caregiver who is extremely patient, forgiving and nurturing. She also carried a lot of pain and sadly seemed to internalize everything.

She went to a residential school as a teen and survived. Her stories of loneliness were the only stories I heard about. When she first started talking about that time, you could see the tears welling up in her eyes and her words were hard to express. She didn't talk about that time to us as children, at least not to me until well into my adulthood. The most vivid pictures that come to my mind from her stories is how she as a shy, gentle young teenager stood in front of a cold stone building far away from her beloved family. She went from a loving home to live in a system that really didn't care for her. To say the least, her self-esteem was severely tarnished, and she never fully recovered from the negative experiences she was subjected to.

The memory she shared first was how after a very long trip on a plane, a train, then a car from Bunibonibee to Portage la Prairie, Manitoba, she was lined up with other Northern kids in front of the Rufus Price building, known then as the Portage la Prairie Indian Residential School. The three-storey brick building was imposing enough for a young girl who had only seen small buildings, houses, and cabins growing up. The tallest building she'd seen until then was a Catholic church with a steeple and bell in Bunibonibee.

She says she was excited but also reluctant to go to Portage and immediately regretted it when she got there. The schoolmaster, Mr. Harris, the head of the residential school in the southern town, came and stood in front of them all as they arrived. Mom says he loomed over them, walking back and forth, asking them questions. One question that she found to be condescending was when he pointed at a car and said where do you think the engine is? She thought, in the front of course! But where she felt the sting of his prejudice and disdain for her the most, she says, is when he walked right over to her and stood in front of her. She was wearing a scarf that her mother made her wear over her head. She says she felt comforted by the scarf, felt a sense of home. As he stopped to stand in front of her, he reached out his hand and ripped the scarf off her head. "We don't wear such things here," Mr. Harris told her, throwing the scarf on the ground. In tears, she recalls that time and says, "It was like he stripped away a piece of me."

The first time my mom recalled this memory to me, those tears and emotions were very intense. Any one of us she told would cry along with her. Including me. She started to explain that what he did to her as a young person who was already lonely, scared and wanting to go home, was strip her of her identity, her self-esteem. He stripped her connection to her mom and exposed her to a harsh new world. This was her first real introduction to the world outside her family. I wish I'd been there to stand with her. In a sense, I feel like I was there. My sweet mom.

Another time she remembers somehow getting a care package in the mail from her mom. "I was so excited to get it," she said. She quickly opened it and found pieces of bannock that she missed so much. Her mother had made it almost every day for them and she hadn't had any since she left home. But when she opened the package further her heart broke because she saw that the bannock was covered in mold. She wasn't crying just because she saw the comfort food destroyed but she was crying because was so lonely for her mom. She felt bad thinking how lonely it must've been for her mom too, at home not knowing how her daughter was. She was hurt and cried for days looking out the windows at empty fields feeling lost and far away.

Another memory she has is being forced to shower with other girls after Residence staff put some sort of powder on her head and body. "They thought we were covered in lice," she said. "Then they cut our hair. They gave me and all the girls a boy's haircut," she recalled. Mom stayed at the residence for about two years before she decided not to go back. During that time, she remembers how hard living there was for everyone, including cousins and friends she had there. She says some of the girls had to physically fight some of the staff to defend themselves and others from abuse and ridicule.

Sometimes, Mom talks about good memories too. Including making new friends at the school and one particularly nice guidance counsellor. She says Betty Ann Caldwell was a good woman who wasn't afraid to show kindness to Mom and other students. Betty Ann made a huge difference in many people's lives. Mom had talked about Betty Ann so many times, I had to help reconnect them. I found Betty Ann in July 2012 living in an apartment on Portage Avenue in Winnipeg, near the Grace Hospital.

I called her and asked her if she wanted to meet my mom again. She agreed and couldn't wait to see her again. Betty Ann invited Mom and me to her apartment and when they saw each other, it was a very sweet moment. They cried happy tears on each other's shoulders as they embraced. "Oh my goodness, you look the same. The same beautiful face," Betty Ann said to my mom. "You too," Mom said as they both giggled. We all had tea and looked at pictures Betty Ann had collected from her time working at the Portage Indian Residence. Many of the pictures included images of young men and women who are now some of

Manitoba's most prominent Indigenous leaders and Chiefs. And she had pictures of my friends Jennifer and Darcy Wood, who had also stayed at the Residence and met there in the 1970s. "She was a firecracker and he was very intelligent," Betty Ann said about Jenn and Darcy.

Our visit with Betty Ann ended with a promise for more visits, but other than a few phone calls and a chance meeting at a hospital parkade, Mom and Betty Ann never visited again. Betty Ann passed shortly after that chance encounter. Mom and I went to her funeral.

As for Mom, she's become a thriver who made the most of life. She raised all of us the best way she knew how and took extremely good care of my dad. She was by his bedside almost every single day Dad was in the hospital in the last years of his life. He did the same for her when she'd end up in the hospital. Mom is still thriving, living in Winnipeg with one of my sisters. My sisters and I live within about five kilometers of each other. Our dad called us kids "Mom's Garden," and we are. Truly.

Chapter 4

LIFE CODE INSTALLATIONS

Brandon and Portage la Prairie are about 126 kilometers apart, but each of those places are about 650 kilometers away from my parents' home communities. All of these places and all of Mom and Dad's experiences have inevitably left an impression on me. Most of it good, but some of it not so good. I was a middle child and I remember being the doer, the chore girl. Of course, my siblings had to do chores too, but I felt like I had more and was the one who was taught to make do with what I had all the time and to help everyone as much I could.

It felt like I had more of the 'hand-me down' clothes. I remember having to go to other people's homes to deliver things or messages for my parents, phones weren't that prevalent at the time. I had to stay back when there wasn't enough room or money to take all of us kids on the plane to go out of town for trips. Don't get me wrong, I don't feel bad in any way about those experiences, I am glad my parents taught me to be helpful, to be a good communicator and to be grateful for what I have at all times. I feel like I still do all these things. Those life lessons have helped me in everything I've done as a parent, a student, a reporter, and as a leader and helped me to work at being humble and mindful of others around me. When Mom and Dad taught me about humbleness, they gave me a gift. It's not always easy, but it's certainly a muscle you constantly have to exercise! I also feel like that's how both my parents were raised. I felt left out of things at times, again for the benefit of others, and I had to be alright with that and I'm pretty sure my parents and others who grew up in the era of Residential Schools and Sixties Scoop must've felt those emotions at times too. I am a descendant of those difficult eras and have learned I have suffered intergenerational trauma from those experiences, much like thousands of others have.

My dad was the oldest of his siblings. One of his jobs as a young boy was becoming an altar boy for a Catholic church and religion became a big part of his life. He never talked to me about his time as an altar boy, but I suspect it was not always an easy time in his life. From that experience, though, he became one of the best Cree translators you'd ever meet in northern Manitoba. Eventually he was recruited to work with missionaries and started travelling with them in their crusades across Manitoba, Ontario and down into the States.

This is how he eventually met my mom. She was home for a few weeks for the summer from Portage la Prairie and a job placement she had as a nurse's aide at the Deer Lodge personal care home in Winnipeg when my dad and the missionaries showed up in Bunibonibee. My dad said when he saw my mom during one of the church services, he knew that she would be his wife. My mom remembered him too and was surprised that her own mom encouraged her to invite him over for supper. After supper, she says he proposed. She said yes, and he left with the missionaries the day after, and she didn't hear from or of him again for a few months. But he had left such an impression on her that she decided not to go back to Portage la Prairie for residential school after that. She wanted to wait for him to return.

It was months later that my mom called for my dad in Cross Lake from one of the only citizens band radio or CB radios, in Bunibonibee. Back then very few people had phones on reserves, radio was available, but not televisions or any other type of signals from outside the community, except for a few CB radios kept at nursing stations. The CB radios were used almost exclusively for emergencies and communicating with people outside the reserve when needed.

Mom was working at the nursing station as a midwife at the time and she was wondering if the man she fell in love with, the man who proposed to her, was actually wanting to marry her. "Are we going to get married? Over," she said, "Yes. Over," he replied. Many people, including those on traplines out on the land who had CB radios, also heard that sweet exchange and the story was recalled every time a wedding anniversary celebration was held! How sweet, telecommunications sealed the deal for my parents.

My dad was always an excellent communicator and speaker. These were just some of the many skills he had that made him a natural leader. He honed his skills in church services, much like some famous singers who say they grew up singing in church, my dad grew up speaking in church. And it wasn't just him, he taught my siblings, mom, and me to do the same. We all had to be prepared at any time to sing or speak in services. But he was the expert, his Cree was on a level that he could translate complicated English terms or ideas into terms any fluent Cree speaker could understand. His example impressed on me to always take speaking in public seriously and to always do so respectfully. To display sound, sympathetic, and well-thought-out arguments and points when called upon or needed. He taught me to be brave and not to be intimidated by crowds when I'm speaking.

Dad was also one who loved to help others but didn't like to rely on anyone for anything to help him, he wanted to be able to provide everything he and his family needed. The people of Bunibonibee, where he wasn't originally from, must've seen that in my dad when he moved there to marry my mom and trusted his ability to lead. In 1971, three years after moving to my mom's community, he was recruited and elected as Chief.

The people in the community relied on him for his strength and ability to say no to government officials when they needed to. In fact, he was one of the first Chiefs in Manitoba and Canada to evict the federally appointed Indian Agent out of the community. And in his first few days as leader, no less! Here's how that story goes: Dad got in as Chief and declared that there wasn't a need to have the Agent in the community since the people had their own leaders. His Councillors agreed with him, and they all went to the house the Agent was staying at in the community. Dad knocked on the door and as the federal government-appointed overseer opened the door, the newly elected Chief (my daddy) and his Council announced to him that he had to grab his belongings and head with them to the airport to leave. "We're here to take you to the airport, you are not needed here anymore," he told the stunned Agent. The Agent initially declined but Dad and the Councillors were adamant that he had to leave. They escorted him to the airport, got him on a plane and told him not to come back. The next day, the Chief and Council waited for a call from the federal government and sure enough it came. "Chief North," a man on the other line said, "what are you doing? You can't kick out the Agent. You can't make decisions on your own, we are sending him back today." Dad replied, "No, he's not welcome here anymore. We can run our affairs. If you send him back, we'll be waiting at the airport and make sure he doesn't get off the plane." And that was that, the Agent was evicted and never made it back to Bunibonibee.

The Indian Agent was one of hundreds across the country assigned to oversee Indigenous people in their own communities. Evicting an Indian Agent was virtually unheard of at the time, but he did it. Dad was a scrapper. His childhood friends told me a few stories about him taking up other people's battles when he was called upon. He didn't seem to be afraid of anyone.

It was a family friend who initially told me about what Dad did in his earlier days as a new Chief. I don't think he realized that what he did was an extraordinary act of sovereignty. Or maybe he was well aware. He was pushing back at the imposition of the federal government's Indian Act policy to manage and govern the lives of Indigenous people so closely by assigning people to keep watch of everyone and everything from right within the communities.

When I did ask him to tell me the story himself, he told me once that he didn't like how the agent was 'treating our people like kids,' that we could run our own affairs. He talked about how he saw the Indian Agent talking to the leaders of the community. Saying 'No' to everything they asked for, including extra plywood so they could make some repairs on their houses. The Agent would say it wasn't a priority. Saying 'No' to people who wanted to leave the reserve to go to an urban centre. It was only when a nurse or doctor said it was necessary for a person to leave that the Agent agreed to let anyone leave, and then only for an agreed period of time.

Before Dad became the Chief, he said he was asked several times by the current Chief and Council to intervene when the Agent became ignorant and dismissive of their requests. "They came and asked me to talk to him," he said. "But he was very rude, and I felt physically threatened by him, so I had to make it clear to him that he couldn't talk to the Chief and Council or me the way he did. We didn't back down from him and he got very mad" he recalled. He said the Agent got so flustered that he threatened to call the RCMP officer in town if Dad kept getting in the way of him talking directly to the Chief and Council. Apparently, Dad told him to go ahead and call the police, but he didn't. The paternalistic and condescending attitude by the Agent to Indigenous people was not unusual. The presence and imposition of having the Agent in the community was a reality for many reserves across Canada for a few decades. It wasn't until the mid-'70s or so that all Indian Agents were removed from their posts on reserves. Though many will say the physical presence of an Agent may be gone, the imposition of government overseers still exists today in one way or another.

Before his first term was up, my dad recruited someone else to run in his place: a woman from the community, Dorothy Grieves. The same woman who'd stand with me at the MKO election as an Elder, forty-two years later. The story Dorothy told me about that time was that my father told her she had leadership skills that were needed and he'd help her lead. "He told me that he wanted to concentrate on raising his family and offered to help me get in as the next Chief," Elder Dorothy told me the day before I was elected as the first female MKO Grand Chief. Dorothy was the first and only woman Chief in our community so far, even until now.

At the time, Dad told me that Dorothy had impressed the community when she was a young woman by hunting and killing large game for her family. "It showed she was a great and brave woman," Dad said. My dad also said he thought it would be better for our young family that he pursued life as an independent entrepreneur where he could make more money. "The role of Chief didn't pay much and I knew I needed to do more to make sure our family could eat," he said. Dad had already taken courses to be a heavy-duty equipment operator before he became Chief. He said his vision was to work with the community by providing the services needed to build roads and other infrastructure.

After helping Dorothy get in as Chief, Dad got to work starting a road construction company that he and my mom operated for more than forty years—right up until he got sick, about five years before he passed away. His main job was building and maintaining part of the winter roads to and from Bunibonibee. He hired workers and they'd be gone for most of the winter working on the roads. The winter road was usually open from early December to mid or late in March for travellers and for suppliers bringing goods for the year. The roads are of course dependent on the weather and are still one of the only ways to get in or out of isolated communities like Bunibonibee. About a third of all reserves in Manitoba for example, have never had permanent roads connecting them to the outside world. These communities are deemed too isolated or too expensive to build roads for. To leave or visit isolated reserves, you'll need to take an expensive plane ride or wait for the winter roads to be built. There are dozens of northern parts of provinces and the extreme north that are still isolated in Canada. I connect this fact again to a lack of political will that keeps these communities in third-world conditions like this. As well, there is a lack of public support or awareness to trigger changes and connect all communities with all-weather roadways.

However, some Indigenous people who live in isolated reserves are okay with their community being closed off to the rest of the world. They feel safer and it keeps them living closer to the land. The feeling of safety became evident when the Covid-19 pandemic hit, and isolated reserves were able to control who was allowed into their communities. The ability to control movements in and out of the reserves kept the coronavirus numbers at bay in the first and second waves, but inevitably the virus broke through the barriers. But at least the communities had a chance to get many people vaccinated before more serious variants of the virus hit.

In more normal years, at least normal for the past few decades, most families wait for the winter roads to open in order to go out for trips outside the community. My parents did the same. It was and still is the most economical way to come and go from the isolated reserves for anyone. Otherwise, you will be paying thousands of dollars for a one-way plane trip per person. And if you're trying to take an entire family, obviously the costs go up. The prices are similar or sometimes cheaper for southerners to go to other countries for vacation or business travel. And as with everything else, travel costs continue to rise.

For a short time after my dad finished his term as Chief and before he became a business owner, he helped many others in different ways. He was a visionary whose priorities were influenced by being raised by his grandparents in Pimicikamak Cree Nation. For example, when he was hired by the Manitoba Indian Brotherhood (the organization that eventually became the Assembly of Manitoba Chiefs), he was asked to identify needs in the community that could be addressed. He and other technicians were tasked to come up with ideas that could be implemented. One of his ideas was for each First Nations community to have personal care homes where elders or people living with disabilities could be assisted and taken care of by their own people, rather than sending them out of the community for care or leaving them in houses they couldn't comfortably live in.

I imagine Dad was remembering what it was like for him and his family to have to live with the fact that his mother was sent away for medical care and never returned. Accepting the fact that she died without a loving family beside her.

Dad also talked about how he was taught to always respect and care for elders. He did and saw the need for that in his own community as a young person. He knew the situation was similar in all reserves. That fact is also still true today. Thankfully, a few reserves in Manitoba do have personal care homes now, including Bunibonibee, due in large part to my late father's advocacy.

I saw my dad and my mom act as huge advocates in our community. Though I didn't realize that when I was a child or even a teen. I just saw it as a normal thing to do, to see them helping or working for others and the community as much as they could. And now for me to do as much as I could. I still have that sense we have to be on call when we're needed, which was the life code they had for all of us.

Mom's gift was her level of hospitality and ability to listen to people who needed to talk. I saw her cry and pray with people many times. She is a natural caregiver and worked as a midwife in our community for a while. She helped deliver a few babies and almost went into nursing full time. Dad supported her dream of becoming a nurse. "One time I was accepted to go to school for nursing and the day I was supposed to leave on the plane, I changed my mind," Mom told us all once. Dad was in the truck with some of us, seeing her off. But just before she got on the plane, Dad said, "She came back and said she didn't want to go. She made a choice to stay home and keep raising you kids." And once in a while, Dad would remind all of us that mom sacrificed her own dreams of becoming a nurse to help us pursue our dreams by being a great mother and support for all of us. Dad used to call us children, "Mom's Garden," especially when Mom would put up pictures of all of us on the wall. He said the wall of pictures was evidence of her garden.

Mom was also our Sunday-school teacher, she had us and other kids on Sunday mornings, sitting in our living room singing songs and listening to Bible stories that she brought to life with pictures and acting out stories in small plays. The other kids who came for Sunday school loved our mom. It was good to be her child.

Mom was a great listener too. She seemed to have someone visiting her all the time. All the while she was there listening to them and counselling them. People loved our mom; she was a source of strength and love for many. She is an excellent example of what a good mother, wife, and friend is. She did such a great job that we as her children see her as the Queen in our family and she gets to see her children working and pursuing dreams. All of my siblings and I are living out dreams we had.

Mom says when we were young, she'd line us up and put her hands on our heads and declare us successful. "This one is going to be a nurse, this one a teacher," she'd say as she went down, declaring us 'blessed and highly favoured.' I vaguely remember that, but I appreciate her words of affirmation. I believe her efforts paid off. With the exception of my adopted brother, my siblings are working in our chosen professions. My adopted brother Harry worked with my dad in construction and he was a great worker. But Harry had trauma he hadn't dealt with before he came to live with us. He was apprehended and sent to my parents. Both Mom and Dad love Harry and did their best to give him a good home. Sadly, the trauma Harry was dealing with never fully went away and he's now struggling to live.

Our childhood wasn't perfect, and I realize we weren't wealthy, but it sure felt like it at times. Mom and Dad made life seem easy. Dad was wise, strong, and kind. But above all he loved Mom dearly. I remember Dad always looking at Mom or talking about her with adoration. Mom loved Dad's sense of humour and would do anything for him. Both of them showed me what it was like to be a loyal partner and companion. They were rarely apart right up until Dad passed in October 2017 and I remember everything he and Mom tried to teach me: to be loyal, to be faithful, to work hard, to be self-sufficient, to share what I had, to take care of myself and my children, to be kind and self-disciplined and to never stop trying to do the right thing. These teachings still resonate with me today and while I don't feel I always get it right, I know I have to keep trying. And I do.

Both Mom and Dad decided to do their best as parents. They avoided negativity as much as they could and were generous with everything they had. I never saw them fight or saw the need for them to say sorry to each other. In fact, I don't remember seeing them mad at each other, or saying harsh words about each other or to us or anyone else. I'm sure they had disagreements, but never in front of me or my siblings. They shielded all of us from any of that. I am grateful for the life they gave me, but I think from that I learned how to avoid conflict and internalize almost everything instead of dealing with negativity in a productive way. I'm not sure exactly where they learned not to complain (I suspect from their times at residential schools, day schools and in church) and why they decided to show me the same, but from that I learned to always 'turn the other cheek.' I can't say living that way was or is easy, but their teachings stayed with me throughout life.

For me though, not complaining and giving everything I had to anyone who wanted anything from me made my life as a teenager, as a young wife, mother and leader harder in some ways and made it difficult to stand up for myself. The biggest way this showed up in my life is in my relationships, including my first real romantic relationship.

I ended up in an abusive relationship that nearly took my life a few times and I was easy prey to predators when I first moved to the city as a vulnerable teenager. I wasn't strong or confident enough to say no to my ex-husband when he was demanding, so he took advantage of me in many ways. I wasn't strong enough to say 'no' to complete strangers who tried to take advantage of me, so I learned to simply avoid situations instead.

The lessons of working hard and making my own way despite the challenges have made a bigger impact on my life than my weaknesses. The strengths I have now have carried me through everything. The ability to keep going even when life gets hard is what my parents helped foster in my life and that serves me well. Now, with everything else I've been taught by my parents, family, and life I feel more resilient than ever, and I am able to accept disappointment easier than some. Life is hard sometimes, but I'm so grateful for the life code placed in me. It makes me stronger every day and helps me to find joy in every stage in life so far, making life easier and lovely in so many ways.

Chapter 5

TRAUMA DRAMA

My early years were very sheltered but bad things still happened to me and my siblings. While my parents always knew where I was, they didn't always know what was going on. I was always outside playing with my siblings and all the neighbourhood kids. Most of the time, playing safely outside all day was the norm. But it was on one of those carefree days with my brothers and sisters that I experienced the first real traumatic thing in my life. A scary event that impacted me negatively for many years.

I must have been about seven or eight. I was with my little sister, my little brother, and two brothers from next door. All four of them were about five and six years old. We were all playing together outside our house when the uncle of the two boys, who was an older teenager, maybe seventeen years old, came to talk to us. In my mind, the guy was already an adult. He was carrying an axe in one hand and looked a little sweaty as he approached us. He was huffing as he started talking to us. He said he had made us a house to play in. We were all excited to hear that. "Want to see it?" he asked.

I shrugged my shoulders, not sure if I believed him.

"Come on," he said. "Follow me I'll show you where it is," he added in Cree. He was pointing towards a wooded area that my siblings and I had never played in before. That alone felt strange.

I remember feeling hesitant and not wanting to follow him but everyone else really wanted to go and I wasn't about to let my sister and brother go by themselves. With huge reservations in my little heart, I trailed behind my younger siblings as they and the other boys followed this guy into the woods.

This guy, still with an axe in one hand, pulled trees back to show us the way onto the path. He let his nephews follow the path, next my sister and brother, then me. He waited to walk behind me.

This wooded area and the path were across the road and away from our houses, away from the safety of our parents' care. Mom or Dad wouldn't have been able to see us from any of the windows at our house if they wanted to. As we got deeper into the woods, the uneasy feeling, my gut instinct to get away from him, got stronger.

We were only a few steps into the woods when all of a sudden, I felt a big wave behind me. He scooped me up from behind and threw me onto the ground. I had no idea what was going on and was extremely frightened. As I lay there struggling to get away, he was pulling down his pants while holding me down with his other hand on my chest. He didn't say anything, but I could hear him breathing and panting over me. He placed the axe next to me and began to take my pants off.

I could see my little siblings on my right side looking down at me crying, scared. The two neighbour brothers were on the left side, snickering and laughing. The guy's big chin and teeth were in my face as he got closer to me and pushed his body on top of my little frame. I remember looking down trying to see what he was doing. As I looked, I saw his ugly penis and immediately tried to push it away from me with my tiny hand. I was so scared, yet I didn't want to scream because I didn't want to scare my little brother and sister even more than they already were. Before he went any further, I heard the guy's mother calling to us. "What are you guys doing in there?" she yelled. "Where are you going?" Thankfully she must have seen us walking into the woods. The guy, her son, jumped up and ran away further into the woods away from us and his mom. He was pulling up his pants as he ran. I got up and pulled up my pants and I rushed my siblings toward the guy's mom. The mom was a very kind-hearted, loving woman. She was always kind to us as kids and as we grew older. So, I was relieved to hear her voice and intervention. I don't know what she knew about her son, but she must've been concerned enough to come and find us. As we walked out of the woods towards her, she saw the three of us crying. "Kona matook," she said, which means, "Don't cry anymore you guys," in Cree. She told us to go home as she led her two grandsons away. My siblings and I ran off as quick as we could without saying a word to her or to each other.

As we walked home my sister and brother were still crying. I stopped as I tried to calm them down. They wanted to go straight into the house, but I kept them outside a little longer. I didn't want Mom or Dad to see them crying. I was worried I'd get them and myself in trouble. I did everything I could to make them laugh and played with them for a while before letting them go inside. I begged them not to tell Mom or Dad what happened. They both agreed. But the second we stepped inside the house, my little brother walked straight to our mom and said, "So-and-so peed on Sheila." I was mortified. I started sobbing quietly. I was so embarrassed and scared. And I was very worried thinking I was in huge trouble.

My mom didn't react right away but soon after my younger siblings settled down, she came and led me into her and my dad's bedroom. We lay down on their bed not facing each other. But all I wanted to do was curl up in her arms. Instead, we lay separately and she asked me to explain what my brother was talking about. With tears streaming down my face and crying as quietly as I could, I started recounting what happened. I was so scared that I was going to get spanked for what happened. But she didn't get mad at me. I'm not sure how she felt actually, but I felt relieved when her reaction was sympathetic instead of getting angry at me. "God is mad at the guy," Mom said. "Not you, okay?" I didn't really understand what she was trying to say at the time, but it helped me feel better. Then she prayed for me and held me in her arms as I cried a little more.

The guy became secretly known for sexually assaulting other kids in the community. We all learned to avoid him. But he managed to assault me twice more as I got older. Thankfully, both times, he was interrupted by other people. And it wasn't just him who sexually assaulted me. Other kids in our community did as well. I'm guessing it was this guy who must've inadvertently taught some kids to do that to other kids. These are some of the early situations of conflicts that I didn't really know how to handle. I felt hurt and vulnerable, but I still didn't feel strong enough to fight back or even speak up for myself. Though I must've found a way to deal with those situations in my own mind because I feel like I was able to get away from sexual bullies before things got worse. In those times, I think my own instincts kicked in.

I also learned to internalize my feelings instead of dealing with them. I felt like the bad things that had happened to me were my fault in some way and I needed to try harder to be good. I wonder if my parents learned that themselves from their times at the Indian Residential School and Day School. I agree with the teaching of 'turning the other cheek' but sometimes it is very hard to do that, especially when turning the other cheek doesn't stop the onslaught of blows that happen when you're being assaulted physically, emotionally, or mentally. In spite of the abuse I suffered as a child at the hands of people outside my family, however, I feel my childhood was the best it could've been. I feel truly blessed for having the parents I have and the siblings I grew up with because my parents made life look and feel hopeful. Hopeful that things will get better, and many times they did, eventually.

Chapter 6

SURVIVORS AND THRIVERS, SURVIVING AND THRIVING

At fifteen years old, I convinced my parents to let me leave home to go to high school in Winnipeg. Both of my older sisters were leaving too, one for university in Brandon, Manitoba, the other for another high school and residence in Teulon, Manitoba. I wanted to go because they were going and I wanted to try doing the higher-level courses that weren't available at our high school. They agreed and I was placed at Daniel McIntyre Collegiate Institute (DMCI) by an agency that worked with our First Nation and found me a place to live with people willing to take students in.

The people I stayed with were nice enough, but it wasn't home. I felt like I was intruding, and nobody really cared if I did my homework, or whether I came home to sleep or eat. I was basically living on my own and that put me in danger several times. Danger because I didn't know anything about living in the city or how to handle racism, bullies and predators.

But what I wanted was more important than what I didn't know: To get into higher level courses so I could go on to university and become a doctor. It was one of the three careers I thought I wanted to pursue. The others were becoming an entrepreneur like my parents and becoming television journalist! I remember how high my excitement level was when I first got to Winnipeg. I was really looking forward to going to school. I loved school, I still loved getting high marks in tests! And I was used to having straight A's and perfect attendance records year after year. Again, not just me but my siblings as well. My parents made sure we did well in school and taught us to take pride in education.

However, just weeks into my first year at DMCI my confidence level as a student plummeted. I couldn't keep up and failed in nearly every course I took. I was used to being one of the smartest kids in class but this time I became one of the 'dumbest' kids in class. I didn't recognize any of the coursework, even though I kept up with the homework. I was too shy to talk to anyone, let alone ask for help with the schoolwork. When I started writing tests and seeing the failing grades, I was devastated. I didn't understand why, and I didn't want my parents to know. A teacher came to talk to me about one of my tests and I didn't know what to say. I was embarrassed. She offered to give me another test, an aptitude test. I agreed and I tested to be two years behind. My reserve school was and still is at least two academic years behind schools in urban areas. In an attempt to do better, I took all of the same courses I took in the first term again, hoping I could bring up my marks. Doing that didn't make much of a difference for me though and I started to fall further behind in schoolwork.

As I was struggling through high school, I also went through a major culture shock being in the city without my family or anyone I knew. I was also so shy that I'd almost cry if you tried talking to me. Because of my shyness, the first few strangers I encountered were intimidating. I can laugh about it now though, but these strangers were fellow transit bus riders. The lady I stayed with took me to the bus stop the first time to show me where it was and which bus to look for. On my first, second, and third rides on the bus I started a routine. I got on and showed the driver my pass like the lady taught me. But I didn't know what to do after that, so I thought I better show everyone that I had a bus pass. In my mind I thought everyone else on the bus had the right to kick me off the bus if they didn't see my pass. To avoid that possibility, I went up one side of the bus then the other, making sure everyone on it saw my pass before I found a seat to sit in! By the fourth bus ride though I caught on and became a pro bus rider.

In Bunibonibee I knew practically everyone, I could stand on the road and if I needed a ride, I could just ask someone passing by to give me one. I remember the first time thinking I could do that in Winnipeg! I tried standing on the side of Portage Avenue in downtown Winnipeg a few times when I first moved to the city. No one would stop, thank goodness. Except this one time. I was at a bus stop wanting to go back to the house I was staying at. It was late and no bus came. I missed the last one. But before I knew that, a total stranger, a man, came up to me and tried chatting me up. Asking my name, telling me how pretty I was and asked if I was cold. I ignored him and ran across the street to get away from him. He followed me and tried to offer me other things like food, a warm place to stay, alcohol, drugs. I never answered him, but he kept pursuing me as I tried to keep ahead of him back and forth on the same street corner. All the while hoping the bus I needed would come. It never did.

Finally, a man in a nice car pulled up to me and asked, "is that man bothering you?"

I said, "yes!"

"Get in the car, I'll drive you home," he said.

Relieved I jumped in, happy to get away from the first older man. We drove off very fast down Portage Avenue, with music blasting. A few blocks down, the man turned the music down and said, "Don't be alarmed but you are driving in a stolen car." Instantly, my relief turned into absolute fear. Everything my parents warned me about was all coming back to me. To be careful, not to talk to strangers. But they didn't mention 'helpful' ones who had other intentions. I had to figure that one out myself.

As we drove toward the place I was staying at, the man said, "I'm from BC and I'm passing through. I just need a place to stay for the night." I told him I didn't have my own place, that I just had a small room. He said he wouldn't mind sleeping on my floor. I told him I couldn't let him in because it wasn't my house. And as if that wasn't bad enough, I took him right in front of the house where I stayed. He put the car in park and said, well I'm going to need a favour for the ride. I didn't know what he was asking for, but I knew it wasn't good. He unbuckled his seatbelt and leaned over to kiss me. As he sat up more to lean in again, I pressed my seatbelt buckle button to let myself free and grabbed the door handle.

The door swung open, and I ran out as fast as I could into the house. I was sure he was right behind me but thankfully I managed to get the door open, and I slammed it shut and ran to my room.

After I made it into my room, I jumped into bed and stayed there for about three days, skipping school. The people I stayed with didn't even notice if I went to school or not and I never told my parents about scary incidents like that because I didn't want them to worry and bring me back to Bunibonibee.

But that wasn't my only brush with almost becoming an MMIW statistic. On another late evening, I was trying to make my way home from hanging out with a fellow classmate. The bus didn't come and I didn't want to ask or rely on another stranger for a ride. I decided to walk home instead of waiting any longer for a bus. As I was walking, I saw a group of young guys in a little car with their windows down, laughing and talking loudly driving up towards me. I heard one of them say, "Hey there's one." I looked over my shoulder to see if they were talking about me. They were. Again, I felt the immense danger I was potentially in. But again relieved because I saw them drive off. Just a few moments later though, I could hear a car squealing around the corner, pulling up fast from a cross street toward me as I ran to hide behind a large stone planter. These guys slowed down to a crawl and I could hear them asking each other where I was, if any of them could see me. Thankfully they couldn't see me and they drove off again.

After they left, I saw a payphone nearby and ran to it and called the one friend I knew who had a car to pick me up. He did. As I got into his car, he gave me a good scolding about not walking around alone after dark. I was thankful he cared. It helped me understand the city and its ways better.

In the second year I was living in Winnipeg, I was placed with another family who lived in one of the poorest neighbourhoods in the city. There, almost every time I left the house to go to the store or catch a bus for school or for any reason, random men would pull up behind or beside me, trying to get my attention. Sometimes it was just cat calls, other times it was to ask me how much I would charge for sex. I never answered them, I just tried my best to get to a safer place. And it didn't matter if it was day or night, the prowlers seemed to always be out looking for young people like myself.

While I was trying to stay away from looming predators, I also faced something that I don't remember ever experiencing until I moved to the city, racism. When I first thought of moving to the city, I thought the streets would be beautiful and clean. That everyone would be nice, fun, and also beautiful. But within days I realized that wasn't the case and moreover I didn't belong in the city. At least that's the feeling that came over me when I first noticed side glances and smirks. I didn't know what the issue was, but I knew it had something to do with me.

Instead of seeing myself as a smart, happy, and determined person, I started to see myself as a shy little Native girl who dressed differently, who talked differently, and who couldn't really relate to anyone. Did I mention I was shy? Partly because my Cree accent would come out once in a while when I spoke! I pronounced 'sh' words with an 'S' for example. Other kids made fun of me because of that and I let them. The kids who became my friends though were also Northern students in their first years. The school had us in the same homeroom so we started to get to know each other. But all of us, it seems, were being marginalized and despised by other students outside of our homeroom. Not by everyone, but by many. Today however, some of those kids in our homeroom have become our leaders and professionals in our community.

These leaders, elected and not, have had to deal with many issues since and they've become amazing advocates for their people. I think as we all got older and became leaders, our experiences from high school helped us learn to adapt to all kinds of situations. Dealing with racism is never easy, but I can say for myself, combatting it over the years has toughened me up. Not that I would ever be grateful to live in a world full of racists, but I am grateful that I now feel that I don't have to put up with that societal problem anymore. I imagine that's how my former fellow classmates feel too, but I can also say it wasn't easy. Being a teenager exposed to racism really takes a hit on one's self esteem. The experiences either drove you to coping in not so healthy ways later in life or drove you to become an advocate in some way for others. Much like the group of students my mom, Jennifer, and Darcy went to school with in Portage la Prairie, the group of students I went to school with found a way to heal and thrive from the negative experiences they were subjected to. Not all of course, but a solid group from each are now some of our most prominent outspoken leaders.

Chapter 7

MY NEW CITY FRIENDS

One friend who protected me from bullies in my first year seemed older and way cooler than I was. She was confident, had a foot-high spikey hairdo and wore clothes that you saw in movies like *Sixteen Candles*. She became one of my new friends after she witnessed fellow classmates making fun of me or saying mean things about me. She stood up for me and told the bullies to shut up and leave me alone. I admired her for that and I'd look forward to seeing her here and there at school. Eventually, we started talking more and she started inviting me to hang out at her house in the North End. I was more than happy to go and visit her, she was fun and made me laugh. While we were hanging out, she would talk about her boyfriend. She talked about how much he loved her and gave her anything she wanted.

At the time, she was living in extreme poverty. Though I didn't see it that way at the time, to me the North End, the poorer end of Winnipeg, was no different than other parts of the city. But then again, I had no idea what the other parts of the city were like at the time either. I mostly stayed in the inner city where I lived or visited the North End.

I trusted everything my new friend said to me and soon after she wanted me to meet her boyfriend. I agreed to meet him. On the day I met him he picked us up at school pulling up in a fancy two-door low-riding candy-apple red Trans Am. I was flabbergasted and super impressed as it pulled up to pick us up at DMCI on our lunch break. Then the driver's side door opened and a man, a much older man, came out to greet us. I was a little confused and thought for a second this couldn't be the man my friend was seeing. I thought maybe the guy was the dad of her boyfriend.

It wasn't, he was her boyfriend, and he was old. Like in his forties! My teen brain thought that was old. My friend was just a teenager herself and

I couldn't understand why she had such an old boyfriend. But she was excited to see him and that put me at ease. We drove to a house not far from our school and hung out in a kitchen that wasn't a normal kitchen. In fact, there was nothing normal about the entire house. All of the windows were covered by cloths, there were old blankets and mattresses everywhere on all the floors through the house, and drug paraphernalia everywhere. I didn't understand what was going on with the house and why it was the way it was. But my friend made it fun and tried to make me comfortable being there. It was a short visit the first time, but the second time another man was there. He was also older, and my friend told me to go with him to another room.

I didn't want to, but I did, my lack of self-confidence prevented me from staying firm and saying 'no' initially. The man I went into a room with could barely speak English, but he knew enough to sit me down and start telling me how pretty I was. He tried to get me to get comfortable and lie down. I did lie down and he started fondling me. I froze but I also felt an immense source of strength and got up to leave the room before he got further under my clothes. My instincts were telling me to get up and get out. I walked straight to my friend and said I had to go. She agreed and we left. I went back to the house with my friend several times and the last time I agreed to go was in the evening. This time, there were other young girls like me there. They seemed to be intoxicated or drugged up as grown men lurked around them, passing some girls around like they were objects. I didn't know what I was seeing but I didn't feel good about it, so I made an excuse and told my friend I had to leave. I told her I was going to meet another friend who wanted to come to the house too. She was okay with that. I didn't though, I just needed an excuse to leave. I went for a walk instead to kill time and made my way back to the house to see if my friend was ready to go. I was hoping she was ready and I'd get a ride home.

When I walked up to the house, the police were there. One of them opened the door ever so slightly and I could see a lot of commotion going on in the house. The cop said, "You don't want to be here, go home." My friend later told me that everyone in the house was being strip searched. For what? I don't even know. But I was sure glad I wasn't there. It was probably the last time I really hung out with my cool new friend.

I heard of similar experiences by other girls who were teens in Winnipeg in the 80s and 90s. Thankfully, I was able to make it out of those situations, but not everyone did. Some ended up going missing, or were murdered, pregnant, or criminally implicated or involved in some way. I realized later that my cool new friend was likely recruited by the older men she was hanging out with to find other vulnerable girls like her to take to the houses these men in gangs ran as brothels.

Still, I was determined to make a go of life in the city, even though I had no family members near me except by phone. It wasn't always easy, but I also made some really good friends outside of school. I didn't really relate to them right away because I felt so different from them. But they were the friends who helped me get through some of those life-changing transitions. These friends had parents that my parents knew of and all of them went to church like my family. They started taking me to youth church services with them and showed me around the fun parts of the city. I am still friends with these people today and I love them dearly.

Chapter 8

DEFENSIVE LOVE

In my second year of high school, when I was sixteen, I met a twenty-four-year-old man whose mother I was placed with by the education authority for my reserve. At the time, the man was serving two years in a medium-security jail. I don't know what he was charged with, my guess is it was for assaulting someone. We got to know each other by phone. When I started living at his mother's, I'd answer the phone once in a while when no one else did. Sometimes it was my house mother's son calling in from jail. From those short conversations we'd talk more regularly. We started planning times he'd call, and I'd be there waiting for the call. I liked talking to him because he was funny and he took great interest in me.

We only met once or twice in person when I would go with his mother and brothers to visit him in jail. He asked me to go with them to see him and I wanted to go as well. When he finally got out of jail a few months after I moved in with his family, we started a relationship that lasted ten years. We had two beautiful children together and I raised them with as much love as my parents showed me. But it was hard at the same time, because this man, the father of my children, the man I loved, was abusive the whole time we were together.

When I met him, I fell in love with his charm and humour. When he got out months later, I fell deeper in love with him as he showed love and adoration. I felt protected and cared for by him, like I hadn't felt since I lived with my parents. He bought me little things and would meet me at school when I was done for the day. But the first honeymoon phase only lasted about two weeks.

The first time he got abusive to me was two weeks after he got out of jail. I went to visit him at his apartment in downtown Winnipeg.

I couldn't stay as long as I usually did, because I wanted to visit my grandpa, Wesley Weenusk, that evening. He was in Winnipeg at the time as an Elder in support of Chiefs during the time of talks about the Meech Lake Accord. I didn't know the significance of the talks at the time, I just wanted to see my grandpa because it had been a while since I'd seen any family from home. But my boyfriend did not want me to leave, and he tried very hard to stop me from leaving. He was very sweet about it at first, asking me to stay. But then he got angry when I told him I really had to go.

At first, I thought it was cute that he was desperately wanting me to stay. But I was adamant that I had to go see my grandpa at his hotel. As I put my shoes and jacket on to leave, he was still asking me to stay. He started to ask more firmly. With my jacket and shoes on and reaching for the door, I tried to reassure him that I'd see him tomorrow. He didn't like that and rushed towards me, very angry, grabbed me by my jacket and pinned me against the wall. I froze. He said, "You're not going anywhere." I moved to try and slip out of his grip. He pushed me even harder against the wall and slapped me across the right side of my face. Not even when bullies surrounded me as a kid back in Bunibonibee and beat me with a bat, did I ever get hurt the way I did that day. No one had ever slapped me across the face like that before!

I stood there stunned, not knowing what to say and not knowing what to do. Little did I know that that was the beginning of the abuse that would last the entire ten years we were together. In the end, I did stay, and I felt guilty for staying because I felt like I was letting my grandpa down. I'm sure he was fine, but I guess what I was sensing was that I was forced to make a choice between my family and this guy. Against my better judgement, I chose him over everyone in my life then and for the years that followed. So much so, school became irrelevant. He didn't like me going there either, so I went less and less. I ended up dropping out of DMCI and got pregnant at sixteen years old.

Being pregnant didn't stop the abuse though. At first it was only slapping and guilt trips. In between those times though, I felt loved and protected. He made me feel like I was the most beautiful person in the world. I felt special because he paid so much attention to me, holding my hand in public, opening doors for me, staring down anyone who looked my way! I described being with him as someone carrying a two-by-four—you came near me you were going to get it. He had me social distancing before it was a thing during the Covid-19 pandemic!

As kids, my siblings and I were never allowed to even see people kissing or hugging on television, let alone allowed to have boyfriends or girlfriends. My brothers were too young then to have girlfriends but even if they wanted to, it wouldn't have been allowed. Being away from my strict parents as a teen in Winnipeg, however, I ended up having my first 'real boyfriend.' It was exciting.

When my ex wasn't fawning over me though, he was angry. It's almost as if he only had two modes. Super loving or super angry. While I was pregnant with our first child, he tried to convince me to move away to Vancouver with him to start a new life. He said he'd get a job there and take care of me and our baby. He tried to convince me that my parents didn't love me, saying they were just trying to control me. He almost had me convinced a few times to cut my ties with everyone I knew and run away with him.

But I couldn't imagine my life without my parents or siblings. So, he stuck it out with me and started controlling my movements and tracking who I talked to in other ways. Before I told my parents that I was pregnant, I was seeing a doctor who gave me the choice of abortion. She gave me every good reason to abort, and I agreed to an appointment. The day I was supposed to get the deed done, my father was in the city and I went to see him at his hotel. Somehow, the doctor's office managed to track me down at the hotel. My new house parents must've told them where I was.

My dad answered the phone and looked perplexed that I was getting a call on his hotel phone. The nurse who called reminded me that I had an appointment, she suggested I get in a cab and get to the clinic. With my dad sitting nearby, I was mortified, hoping he couldn't hear the conversation. The nurse was trying very hard to convince me that ending the pregnancy was for the best. I finally had to say I wasn't going. She was disappointed and told me to call them back to reschedule. I didn't, and eight months later I had my beautiful baby girl on Christmas Day.

When I did finally tell my parents, they immediately yanked me back home to Bunibonibee. No more school—I wasn't going anyway. The schoolwork was still hard, and I didn't feel confident that I could get into university with the marks I was getting. Besides that, all my attention was focused on my baby's father. Our relationship changed, of course, because it became a long distance one. He stayed in touch though, he would call me often and send me gifts. I fell deeper in love with him, and I missed him dearly. I wanted to go back to Winnipeg to be with him, so I sought out and found Lindenview, a home for pregnant teens and what they called, 'unwed mothers.'

I begged and pleaded with my parents to let me go there. I told them I wanted to finish school, but really, I wanted to be with my boyfriend. They did allow me to go but only after they voluntarily gave me over to the child welfare system so the system could pay for my stay at the home. The home was nice. I met other pregnant teenage girls. We all had our own rooms to keep clean and a cafeteria where we all ate together. The staff were really nice too. During the day I went to a small room where we did high school courses through distance learning. It was an option. The other option was to go to a high school nearby the home. My boyfriend wouldn't have it; he said he didn't want me to meet other guys there. Ha!

It was at our little classroom where I learned to type. I remember thinking at the time that I should learn to type so I could eventually get a job in an office. At least I had future aspirations. My boyfriend was allowed to visit, but only in one room where our visits were monitored and short. Needless to say, he never hit me or got really mad during that time. After all, he still knew where I was at all times. So, I was safe and enjoying my time with the other girls and getting big.

I was due to deliver my baby on January 1st that year. Leading up to Christmas, I asked my parents and the supervising staff to allow me to stay with my boyfriend over the holidays. They allowed it and I went to stay at his little place downtown. We were in sweet bliss, in love more than ever. We made meals together, watched movies, and he treated me like a queen. About six a.m. Christmas morning, I started to feel intense cramps on my back. The process was starting. My baby was on her way, though I didn't know if we were having a girl or boy at that time. It was an exciting time, even though it was painful.

My boyfriend came with me to the hospital and he kept my parents up to date on the progress of my labour. It took all day but finally around seven that evening, as my family back home were eating Christmas dinner, I delivered our baby girl. We called my mom right away and we could hear the house full of my relatives yelling 'congratulations.' I could tell my mom was crying when we called, so was I. Seeing my baby girl's little face took me to another realm in life. Until that moment, I never really understood what it was like to love someone. This little baby taught me that as soon as I saw her face and heard her cry. And, I have to agree with the saying that all the pain stops as soon as you see your baby after they're born. That happened for me too.

A few days after she was born, we were released from the hospital. I really wanted to go back to my boyfriend's place, but I wasn't allowed by my parents, so I had to go back to the home. What was super cute though, was that the nurses put my baby and all the other babies born that week in giant Santa stockings. I wish I had a picture of that, though I do in my head. When we got back to the home, I graduated to the basement floor where other young moms who delivered and kept their babies stayed. We had our own kitchen and washrooms, so I felt really grown up. Especially because I had to start buying my own groceries and cooking my own meals. I continued to take classes and my baby was cared for by volunteer grannies who came to sit with our babies. My baby was a favourite for the ladies because she always seemed to be happy and the easiest to take care of. She was a sweetheart.

Eventually, after being taught how to budget and cook for myself, the staff at the home helped me find an apartment to move into with my baby. I felt really blessed and I thought my life was going to be easy after that. I was wrong. Days after I moved into my new one-bedroom apartment, my boyfriend brought all his things over and moved in. I actually didn't want him to. I wanted to honour my parents and at least not 'live in sin' with him. I told him that, but he thought that was ridiculous. I kept trying to stand my ground and say we couldn't live together because we weren't married. Inevitably, those talks got him agitated and he started lashing out.

My parents knew he was staying over a lot too and they started telling me to "just get married then." I didn't want to, but I also wanted to do the right thing. My boyfriend, on the other hand, was getting forceful about staying over. He wanted to stay with us. But I remember feeling then that though I enjoyed his visits, I wanted our baby and I to have the place to ourselves and to keep going to school. I reminded him we couldn't live together because we weren't married. I thought the idea of getting married would deter him. Eventually, he said, "let's just get married then." The proposal of a lifetime!

I gave in and eight months after my daughter was born, the three of us flew to Bunibonibee to get married. We got married at the same time my parents were hosting gospel services under a big-top tent. While we were there for those few days, we were good. No fights, no abuse. My ex was a perfect gentleman and we had fun. I see pictures of that day now and see how young and naïve I was. I was barely eighteen years old. It's not unusual for eighteen-year-olds to get married, especially back then. But I feel I was way too young then, especially since I wanted to pursue my dreams. Doesn't matter now, I got married to make sure everyone was happy. The wedding day was a perfect, beautiful sunny warm day in August. We took pictures by the lake with all my bridesmaid sisters. My parents ordered lots of food and we feasted with many people who were also there for the gospel services.

I remember the cute dress I was wearing. I only had $200 to find a dress for myself. With my little girl in tow, I went to a dress shop. This was a shop in downtown Winnipeg on Vaughn Street near Portage Avenue, by The Bay building. I remember the shop so well because I saw it often when I was going to high school and catching buses right in front of the building. I used to dream about going inside to try on dresses.

When I first walked in and told the attendant that met me at the door my situation, she let out a big sigh and said, "Come on, I only have one dress for you." She brought out this cute little dress made of lace. I tried it on as my little girl crawled around under the expensive dresses in the main showroom. Thankfully, the little lace dress fit perfectly. Like it was made for me. The attendant and I were so happy, at least that was my impression of her. Maybe she was just happy to get me and my cute crawling baby out of there. Nonetheless, that was when I said 'yes to the dress.'

Our marriage lasted for eight years. After the wedding, we went back to Winnipeg, but neither of us was working and tensions got high when we ran out of money for things. One time, our fight was loud enough for the police to come to our apartment. They came in and separated us. One officer took me and my baby into our bedroom. He asked me if my husband hit me. I lied and said 'no.' Well, "Quit making all the commotion or we'll take you to jail and have social workers come get your baby," he said. That was unpleasant! I'm not sure what they told my ex, but he smartened up for the night after that.

We were only in my little apartment for about three months after we got married. My dad offered my husband work on the winter roads back home. He really wanted to go, and I encouraged him to go. I was looking forward to living away from him for a while, thinking that would make both of us happier. But he wasn't having it. He had us pack up our clothes and literally had us crawl out a window to leave my little place in the middle of the night. I had to leave all the first pieces of furniture I ever bought for myself. It was all used furniture, but it was still mine and I was pretty happy to have it all. All we took was our clothes and personal items like pictures and paperwork. But my husband didn't want me to stay in the city by myself. He accused me all the time of cheating on him or that I would cheat on him. He didn't trust that I wouldn't cheat on him if he left and I stayed behind.

I felt horrible for leaving our first apartment like that though, because I was skipping out on my lease and I knew it would make the people from the girls' home look bad because they vouched for me. My ex didn't care and I felt I had no choice but to leave. Sure enough, the landlord and the people who vouched for me tracked me down at my parents' weeks later. But it was too late, I didn't have any control or the means to fix the problem my leaving caused. All I could do was apologize to everyone.

When we did move to Bunibonibee, we had to live at my parents' place, the home I grew up in. Mom and Dad gave us one of the three bedrooms and it got very crowded because my younger siblings and a baby nephew were living there also. Tensions got high between my ex and me there too, but I kept his abuse hidden and I complied fully with him. I didn't want my parents or anyone else to see any of it. I must've hidden it well because my parents thought we were the happiest couple. In some ways we were, we were in love, and we loved our baby girl, Trisha. Within weeks of moving home I got pregnant again. Life had glimpses of getting better. My husband loved to work, and he was a hard worker, impressing my dad. That made my husband happy too. All seemed to be going in the right direction for us, especially when we found our own place to live in the community. It's very rare to find empty houses on reserves, especially ones that are habitable and available. Thankfully one of my aunts-in-law's sisters was renting her old house and we were there at the right time to get it. A tiny little house but I appreciated it.

We were so happy to move in, but the honeymoon phase didn't last long. As we started living alone, tensions grew again. I can't even say why, I just remember feeling like I was walking on eggshells all the time. And it didn't seem to matter that I had a growing child in my big belly, my ex still got mad and threw me around like I was a lifeless doll. I remember flying across the room several times and me holding my belly as I fell.

One of saddest memories from that time is when my little girl was just over a year old and I was still pregnant. Maybe about seven months pregnant. My ex was yelling and hitting me in the room and all I wanted to do was go see where my little girl was to see if she was safe. She was still a baby herself and didn't really know how to talk yet. I rushed out of the room and ran to the living room as my ex followed me and pushed me forward as I was walking. I fell forward but caught myself before my belly hit the ground. I looked over and there was my little girl, on the edge of the couch that was right against a big picture window. She was sitting on the back of the couch pressed against the window and sobbing quietly. She was so tiny, so scared. I felt heartbroken to see her sitting there like that, so much so it didn't matter at that moment what else was going on and what he was doing to me. I just let him finish yelling, not fighting back anymore. I just wanted to hold my baby girl and comfort her. She didn't deserve to hear and see all that. But she did.

After every fight, my ex would either come cry to me and be super apologetic about physically hurting me or he'd be matter of fact and say

I should 'know better.' He even had me convinced that every time he hit me or yelled at me, it was about 75 percent or more my fault. Not sure why or how he came up with that, but it was a common argument for him. The entire time we were together—aside from the time I lived at the girls' home—I constantly had bruises somewhere hidden around my body. One never fully healed before I got a fresh one. The longest time I went without being kicked, punched, or slapped was about two weeks. I remember because the one cousin who knew I was being hit asked me once "When is the last time he hit you?"

"Oh, a long time ago," I said.

"How long?"

"I can't even remember, maybe two weeks?"

Saying that shocked me and my cousin, I realized how ridiculous it sounded. So did he! But I still didn't leave him.

When it was time to deliver our second child, we had to go wait in Winnipeg to be close to a hospital. Most pregnant women and girls living on First Nations had to leave their homes and deliver babies in an urban centre close to them. It's still that way today.

In the city, we went to stay with his mom and as soon as we got there, my husband disappeared. He was gone for days while I waited to have our son. To this day I still don't know where he went and who he was with. I was concerned of course, but there was nothing I could do to find him or even reach him. The day he did come back, I wasn't allowed to ask where he was.

I could tell he was high or hungover when he finally came back. Of course, I was concerned but not enough to potentially get slapped for questioning him, so I didn't ask. Instead, I focused on getting this baby out safely and keeping our little girl safe. The day our son was born was another beautiful sunny day. My ex came with me to the hospital and we were very happy and excited. One of my sisters just started living in the city during that time too and looked after our little girl while I was in the hospital.

My ex stayed with me the whole time but the moment he had to leave the hospital, my son arrived. We had waited since about seven a.m. that day, then as soon as my husband left the room, around three p.m., my new little baby was born, Sonny. Again, all the pain I felt up until I delivered disappeared as soon as he was born. I was over the moon to see this little boy. My heart was full of love and I didn't care that my husband wasn't there. He was running an errand.

After leaving the hospital, I asked my sister if we could stay with her because I didn't want to chance being alone again at his mom's if we went there. My sister welcomed all of us and we stayed a few days. About a week after having my son, my ex wanted to have sex. He knew it wasn't recommended because I was still healing from delivering our son. It didn't matter, he wanted what he wanted. So, we had sex and then he left right after for the night leaving our two babies and I at the apartment alone. My sister was gone as well, at school. Everything seemed fine until I started bleeding profusely.

My little girl was still barely talking then and was still so tiny and of course my son was just a newborn. I was getting worried because the bleeding got so bad that I sat on the toilet hoping it would stop. I started to feel weak, and I knew we needed help. I couldn't call anyone to come sit with us either and I certainly couldn't call my husband. I didn't know where I would be able to reach him. Besides that, the cordless phone was unreachable for me. But I had to do something, my son was starting to wake from his nap and I couldn't go pick him up or even see if he was okay.

As I sat on the toilet, blood gushing out, I talked my little girl through getting me the cordless phone. It took a while, but my smart little angel understood what I was asking her and eventually brought the phone. She was so smart, still is. When she handed me the phone, I called 911 right away. The ambulance came quickly, arriving just as my sister was getting home. The paramedics had their stretcher and were beginning to strap me in to take me to the hospital. I was hoping somehow, they could fix the problem right there so I wouldn't have to leave my babies. No such luck, they said I had to go to the hospital. Thank goodness they let me take my newborn though. I couldn't leave him because I was only breastfeeding him at the time. They laid him down on my left leg. I kept my hand on him as we got carted off. My little girl was worried, but I knew she'd be okay with my sister. My sister and I talked to her to make her laugh so the situation wouldn't seem so bad. She was okay but

I was crying as we got wheeled away, I felt like I was dying inside. I was embarrassed for some reason that this happened. I didn't tell anyone but the doctors until now how the bleeding started.

The doctor found tears inside my cervix and had to repair them. I stayed in the hospital for a few days to heal. Meanwhile, my husband was nowhere to be found and at this point I didn't care. I just wanted my kids to be okay. Eventually he did come back, and we all went back home to Bunibonibee. I don't know what he did while he was gone, and I was never allowed to ask about it. At this point I wanted out of the relationship. I just wanted my kids to be safe. But that didn't happen for a while yet.

Instead, we started living at home in Bunibonibee again. We found a bigger place to live in because the other family needed the tiny house back. When we got there my husband started working at the Northern Convenience store across from our house. He started meeting new people. People who were involved in drinking and smoking up. None of it was allowed in our dry community but somehow, he found people who had access to drugs and alcohol and he started hanging out with them. He was still good to our kids for the most part though. He did get impatient with them sometimes but mostly impatient with me. He wanted to do what he wanted without question.

I remember opposing his leaving the house once. I wanted him to stay with us. I didn't like the idea of him doing drugs or drinking alcohol. I was never a part of any of that growing up. For the most part he kept it away from me, but he'd leave to do all that. And whatever else he was doing or who he was seeing. I wanted him to stay because he still had great qualities about him that made me and our kids feel special and he made us laugh.

That night he did stay, and we put the kids to bed. But as soon as the kids fell asleep, he led me to the living room and sat me down on the couch. He sat on the floor in front of me. He had five-pound dumbbells on the outside of both my feet. He asked me what my problem was and said he could do what he wanted. I suppose he was offended that I asked him to stay and that I didn't like him hanging out with the people he was hanging out with. I also asked him not to do drugs or drink alcohol. As he sat in front of me with his legs folded and my feet and the dumbbells between his legs, he looked up at me. He fixed his eyes on mine. I looked into his eyes too and they seemed like they were glowing and it sounded like he was growling underneath his breath. It was intense. He asked me again what my problem was as he picked up one of the dumbbells, smashed my right foot with it, and put it back down, still staring into my eyes.

I can't really explain the pain I felt on my foot, but I can remember it felt like it was on fire. I didn't know what else he was going to do, but he had a look in his eyes that made me sit very still. I relented and didn't say anything else. He put the weights away and walked out of the house. My foot swelled up like a balloon and I couldn't fit any shoes on it for a few days. I think one or some of the bones were broken because I couldn't walk on it properly for weeks. But I never had it checked out, it was just easier that way.

Another time, I remember him coming home from work one day. He was very mad about something and I knew it wouldn't be good for me and the kids. I led the kids into a room and had them playing as I shut the door. Every time I sensed my ex getting into a mad state, I'd do my best to occupy our children so they wouldn't see or hear what was happening. I'm not sure if I ever really fully shielded them from the violence but I had to try.

When I went out of the room to see what my husband was doing, he was in the kitchen slamming things as he made something to eat. I was trying to avoid him but also checking to see if he calmed down. Nope, he was still mad. He grabbed me by my hair and made me sit down on the kitchen floor on my knees. He was yelling at me about something that I can't even remember. As I sat there, trying to talk calmly to him, he opened the fridge and calmly started to pull condiments out and put them on the table as I sat there.

After he slammed the fridge shut, talking loudly, he turned to focus on me as he started to empty each bottle one by one on my head. Mustard, ketchup, pickles, juices, anything that could be poured, he poured it on my head and threw the empty containers against the wall. I tried to get up once, but he wouldn't let me and swore at me to stay where I was.

I sat there looking at the floor as he stood there yelling obscenities until we heard a noise at our back porch. We both heard it and he darted off into one of the bedrooms as I sat there with all the condiments streaming down my face and body. The door opened and I looked up to see one of my aunts. At first, she came in cheery but got quiet as soon as our eyes met. She made a stunned face. She didn't say anything, she just kind of backed up and left. It was super awkward. I felt humiliated sitting there. After she left, I quickly got up and cleaned up the kitchen so no one else would see it. It was just another day after that.

A day later though, my aunt's husband stopped in to talk to me. He was a social worker. "Are you and kids okay?" he asked me.

"Yes, everything is good," I said. "I made him angry and we had an argument."

"Did he hurt you or the kids?"

"Mots, no" I answered. And technically he didn't hurt me physically that night nor the kids. Though he did psychologically.

"Okay, but you know you don't have to put up with anyone hitting right?" he said.

I nodded yes and he got up to leave. I played it off trying to convince him that nothing was wrong. I know he didn't believe me but there was nothing else he could do about it. I was protecting my husband and that was that.

Another eventful day was when my ex decided to talk to me again after our kids went to sleep. I wasn't sure what he was going to do but it felt very evil. He led me to the back of the furnace room this time. He had me stand there as he started to unpack a gun my dad had given him to shoot geese with. As soon as I saw what he was doing, I had to do something. I didn't want him to shoot me and scare the kids.

I was going to turn around and leave but I didn't want him to come after me and wake up the kids. Instead, I just stood there and the room started to feel really small. For a minute I thought about faking fainting, but then I really did! The next thing I knew, he was standing over me with the gun in his right hand yelling at me to get up. I did get up and I think it must've shocked him too because thankfully he put the gun away and that was that. We never talked about it again. I'm not sure what he was actually planning to do with the shotgun, but I did feel like all of our lives were in danger. My body felt weak and I was sweating afterward. I didn't have a good sleep that night.

One of the last times we had an argument while living in Bunibonibee was one payday when he decided to leave us and go to Winnipeg. He said he wanted to go visit his mother. "I need to go see her; I miss her. And I want to get more into boxing while I'm there," he said. I was more than happy to hear he was leaving because I had had enough, for now. He took his whole paycheck and said he needed mine too. Knowing that was all the money I had, I went to cash it and gave it all to him anyway. I just wanted him to go and stay away as long as he could. I was planning my next move.

He left and as soon as he did, I started calling the women's shelters that I found in the phonebook. I needed to know if any of them had room for me and my kids because I planned to get out of Bunibonibee, go to a safe place, and find a way to set up a life somewhere for myself and my little kids. While I was waiting for calls back, I started selling off all our furniture and ended up making up for all the money I gave my ex when he left. It only took me a few days to sell all that we had, and I told my parents we were all leaving as a family to go back to the city. I told them my husband had gone ahead to find us a place. I didn't want them to know or worry.

They didn't question us leaving as I packed up my kids and left. One of the first shelters I called was in Thompson, Manitoba. Thompson is the closest urban centre from our reserve, a little city our parents took us to for vacations when my siblings and I were young. Dad'd take us there for most March breaks after he was done building the winter road. It was about a half-hour ride by plane to get there and about seven hours to drive there by winter road, though Thompson is only about 186 kilometres from Bunibonibee.

From there, the people at the shelter bought us bus tickets and we went down Highway 6 to Winnipeg, about 760 kilometers down south from Thompson. Coincidently, my mother-in-law at the time was working in the shelter I was being set up with in Winnipeg. She had a troubled past too, but she loved me and the kids. She helped us. "Awe my girl," she said when I first saw her as she kissed and hugged each of us. "You're going to be okay; I won't say anything about you being here," she added. I asked her if she actually saw him. "Yes, he is staying at my place," she said. She assured me that she wouldn't tell him anything, saying she knew how angry he got. She kept her word and we stayed at that shelter for a few days.

My big plan was to eventually end up in Brandon. Brandon is just over 200 kilometers west of Winnipeg. My eldest sister went to university there when we all left for school as teenagers. It seemed like a nice little city. And ultimately I wanted to live there with my kids because I knew it was a good place for people who wanted to attend post-secondary school. I wanted to be there, so I could eventually go to university or college there and raise my kids in peace. Before long, space for us opened in Brandon and we made the move.

Chapter 9

BRANDON

When I first moved to Brandon with my little kids, I was excited. I felt the same flutters in my stomach as I did when I first left Bunibonibee as a teen to live in Winnipeg. I was hopeful and I felt like I could do anything once I set myself up.

The staff at the shelter in Brandon were nice and they treated my kids and me well. But the place wasn't homey, it was very institutional and cold—not a place you wanted kids to be for a long period of time, or me as a woman fleeing an abusive relationship. One of the things the intake worker stressed with me was that I could only stay there for a month. After that, I had to leave no matter what. I took that as a challenge and began looking for places through listings in the paper. I made appointments to see places, with my kids in tow. We walked to almost every apartment we went to see. There weren't that many places available for rent then. Not ones I could afford anyway. The ones I could, didn't seem safe for us.

The vacancy rate in the western Manitoba town was always low because it was a school town, many students taking all the affordable places. I didn't really realize what that meant until I tried to find a place myself. I swear I searched every day, sometimes almost all day. It became a mission, and I exhausted myself looking because I was keeping the month deadline in mind. As the month deadline approached, I was in a panic. I went to the intake worker and cried in her office. I felt like a failure. I don't know what I was hoping for from her, but to my surprise and relief she said, "It's okay, you can stay a little longer."

Those words gave me such relief and I was able to sleep better that night. But I didn't give up on my search. For weeks we were essentially alone until the only person I knew in town, a friend of one of my sisters, tracked us down and came to visit us. She, Heather Hutton, became a really good friend and spent a lot of time with us, driving us to places we needed to go. I am still so grateful to her.

One day she offered to take us to see a place I found on 'North Hill.' North Hill in Brandon is not far if you have a vehicle, but it seems like it is out of town when you don't. At least it did for me. The place I saw was a former motel. The suites were just one long room with a small kitchen, a bathroom, and very dark wood panel walls. The owner saw me and my small children and I knew she was about to say no, she couldn't rent it to us. Before she could, I begged her. "Please," I said. "I just need it for a month, that's it. I'll keep looking for another place," I added.

"This is really no place for children, it's really for single adults," the landlady said.

I told her my kids and I would be quiet.

Reluctantly, she said 'yes.' I must've sounded desperate. Maybe it was the stress of looking and not finding anything for what seemed like forever, but I cried. I felt so elated and relieved.

The apartment wasn't anything special. It was far from everything; we hardly saw anyone and it felt like we were sitting in a box. The windows seemed very high maybe because I only had a mattress on the ground to sit and sleep on. But we made it homey and we felt safe there, just the three of us. Heather was our only visitor and we loved it every time she stopped by. The memories and feelings I felt at that time are still so clear to me. Maybe it was because I was in a vulnerable state and I thrived on every bit of kindness that I came across. I was appreciative and I felt I could go far even with just a drop of hope.

Even in the struggle to get things we needed, there was kindness in the most unlikely places. But I didn't see it the first time I went to the foodbank to get bread. I still had money from my furniture sale in Bunibonibee, but I was scared to spend it because I knew I needed to keep it for a new place I was hoping to get. And to get furniture and other things we'd need for the house. To make ends meet, I went to a local foodbank that the shelter told me about before I left there.

With my son in a snuggly and my daughter in her stroller, we lined up with others outside the small building to see what they had. As soon as the door opened, it was a free-for all. People in the line pushed each other and us to get the best stuff. I didn't know what to think, I was more surprised than anything, I guess. I had never been to a foodbank before, and I had never seen people rush to grab food like that. But I did get some bread and went back there one more time after that.

The second time I went was different; I still had my son in a snuggly and my daughter in a stroller. We stood around the corner, hidden a bit, waiting for the rush to end. I had decided to just wait until the rush was done before going inside. My strategy was to wait, grabbing what we could and leaving as fast as we could.

As I stood there, a woman sitting in a truck across the street at the Greyhound Bus depot stared at us. It got a little uncomfortable because she stared so long before she got out of the truck and walked straight towards us. With her husband behind her looking onward, she reached her hand out to me and asked, "Are you waiting to get bread?" I said, "yes." I thought I was in trouble. Instead, she was trying to give me something in her hand. I looked and it was $20! She said, "Here, go buy some." Oh my God, my mind was blown. She completely surprised me. I thanked her profusely and left quickly. I bought a few things and went home feeling amazing. She will never know how her $20 made me feel like a millionaire! The only way she'd know that is if she ever felt someone show her kindness the way she showed us that day. And I suspect she did by her gesture.

This woman and Heather reminded me what it was like to be human. I was motivated to keep going, to keep trying to make my life better for the kids and me. Eventually, I started to venture out more into the little big town. I found myself at the Brandon Friendship Centre. They had a soup kitchen and I took my kids there as a treat. We met other people and the kids had a chance to play with other kids. It was there that one of the staff members told me about low-income housing available for Indigenous families. I immediately began the process of applying for one of the houses. To my surprise they had one for me because I was fleeing an abusive relationship. The waiting list they said was typically about six months to a year. But because I was leaving an abusive relationship, they got me into one within weeks of when I applied. The house was a gift, another kind gesture that made me hopeful for our future.

This split-level duplex on 6th Street felt like a mansion. It was perfect. I still had some of the money I made from selling my furniture in Bunibonibee and I saved it to buy me and the kids beds, a table, and a couch. All used stuff, but new to me. I started to feel better, stronger, safe. We met our neighbours and became fast friends. The woman and her kids were in a similar situation to ours, fleeing an abusive relationship.

We were about six months in and enjoying our new place. Of course, that's what it felt like to me, my kids did seem happier, but I can't imagine what it must've been like for them to not have other family around. We were safe and there was no one getting mad in the house the way their father used to. But I did feel sad for them because I was used to having many family members around as I grew up. Here it was just us and we didn't have much.

On my son's second birthday I bought one of those tiny circle cakes at Safeway and a hard plastic Barney squeeze toy. He loved Barney at the time. I set his little cake up with a candle and my daughter with me, we sang happy birthday. It was a great feeling to see them smiling, especially when I presented him with the small Barney toy. He grabbed it and kissed it. I can still see the picture I snapped with a disposable camera, in my head, a precious time. I took a lot of pictures of my kids, always have. So did my mom when we were kids. We still have many pictures from both those times, me as a kid and my kids as they grew up.

This is a happy memory, but I also remember starting to feel lonely. As I started to feel settled and secure, I reached out to my mother-in-law to see how she and my husband were doing. She said he was lonely and was distraught not knowing where we were. I immediately felt sorry for him. She asked to put him on the phone and we talked. He started crying. So did I.

I didn't tell him right away where we were, but we stayed in touch. He called several times a day, being as charming and loving as ever. He told me things I wanted to hear, and the kids loved talking to him too. About two weeks in, I gave in and told him where we were. That same night, he hopped on a Greyhound bus and came to see us. We were all very excited and happy to see each other. We were entering another beautiful honeymoon phase. I loved it. It was about nine months since we'd all seen each other last.

A few days into his visit, he asked to move in permanently. Again, I wasn't sure about that, I was hesitant, and I used the excuse that my landlords wouldn't allow that because I was there on an emergency basis. Which I was, and sure enough the landlords confirmed that he couldn't move in until there was proof he was reformed.

My husband's answer to that was moving to Brandon and entering a temporary live-in program at the Addictions Foundation of Manitoba. "I know I need to change, and I want to. I applied to get into treatment at AFM in Brandon. So, I'll be going there for a few weeks. After that, I'd like to move in," he said. I liked that idea and that's what he did. He said it was his addiction to marijuana that made him act like a jerk! I didn't know anything about that then, but I supported him. I was never around alcohol or drugs as a child, and I didn't want my kids to be around any of that either. And they weren't. Not that I know of anyway.

When my husband finished the treatment program my landlords allowed him to move in with us and he did. It was bliss because our family was intact again. He was back to being the perfect guy. He helped me keep the house clean, he took excellent care of the kids, and he cooked. He was always funny and fun. I started to feel better about myself and started to look for ways to get into college.

During that time, I also took the opportunity to seek medical treatment for my painful hips. My hips had a burning painful sensation every day and all day ever since I could remember. And it seemed to get worse, though I didn't let the pain stop me from doing what I needed to do to take care of my family. But since I was now near medical resources, I decided to see what if anything could be done to stop the pain.

It took months but finally a doctor referred me to an orthopedic surgeon and he suggested I have surgery to temporarily fix the problem. He said my hips needed to be replaced because the sockets and hip joints were out of line and rubbing against each other. He said I was too young for hip replacements and he offered to at least adjust them so the bones didn't rub together. I agreed and I was slated for my first surgery in Winnipeg about a year after we moved to Brandon.

The time after surgery was brutal. I stayed flat on my back for two weeks in the hospital when it was done because we were waiting for a hip brace to be delivered before I could be discharged. My parents were in Winnipeg at the time, visiting my sisters so they were able to take care of my kids while I was in the hospital. My husband stayed behind in Brandon, working.

When I was finally discharged and got back to Brandon, I had to use crutches for a couple of months along with a massive metal brace covered in pink cloth (my choice of colour) that looked like one of those wrestling or boxing championship belts with a hip holster but worse and uglier! Even though it was pink. It went all around my waist and down to my knee on my left side. However, I was very grateful, hoping the pain would be gone forever on the one side. The surgeon suggested I get the other one done a year after the first one.

One day, while in my hip contraption, I made my way to the library by bus for one specific book. I had a plan. Since I couldn't really go anywhere or work, I decided to study the massive general educational development (GED) book I found at the library. It was as big and heavy as a phone book from the '90s. I brought it home and studied it religiously from front to back, every page. I took all the practice tests in it. My intention was to study it and do the exam, pass, and use the certificate to get into college. And that's exactly what happened. I did every quiz in the book and scheduled to do a test in Winnipeg about three months later.

I passed; I still have the tiny diploma. I framed it. Before I got into college as a mature student though, the problems we had as a couple started again. My husband started going out again and staying out longer and longer. Of course, I wasn't allowed to ask what was going on, but I did anyway. He still didn't like it and started to treat me the way he used to before we broke up the first time.

Once when he came home from an excursion, I sensed he was angry. Thankfully, the kids were sleeping. I went to our bedroom, thinking if he hit me and I fell, at least I'd have a safer place to land on my bed. I was still wearing my hip brace and using crutches. He came in the room and I had wedged the bottom of my brace on the bed and held tight on the crutches as he came at me. He slapped me across the face and was yelling, telling me how ugly I was. "What is your problem," he asked me. "You think I need to answer to you? You can't even walk, you're disgusting, you're fucking ugly. You think I want to stay here and look at that?" he asked, pointing at my hip.

I did feel ugly. And worse, because I knew my kids were in the next room. I was hoping they couldn't hear. At this particular time, he was more mad than usual. He grabbed my open Bible on a dresser and started ripping pages out and biting them. My Bible reminded me of being home with my parents and reading it made me feel close to them and to God. Seeing it nearby when I'm going to sleep comforts me and he knew how much it meant to me. Especially this one that my dad gave me with my name embossed in gold on the cover.

I couldn't understand why he was doing that but I was scared for sure. When he was done, I think we just cleaned up the room and went to bed. Got up the next day, acting like nothing was wrong.

But things got worse. The anger and abuse became the norm again. At one point just like he had done that one time in Bunibonibee, he made me sit on the floor in front of him in our dining room while he dumped any condiments he found in our fridge on my head. He had just flipped me around the room by my hair and slammed me on the ground near my kids' toy area. I just sat there on my knees, surrounded by toys sobbing quietly as he dumped the food on my head. I felt like a dog. I just wanted him to finish what he wanted to do and let me go. When this storm passed, things went back to normal again. I accepted that it was 80 percent my fault that it happened, I apologized. He did too and we went back into a honeymoon phase.

The honeymoon phases became less and less appealing though. My love for him started to diminish. At the same time, I started to think about what I could do to get away from him for good. But I felt I needed to get a good job, one that needed a diploma of some kind to get. I applied for college and got in as a mature student with my GED. I was pumped and poured myself into going to school and worked hard for every grade I got. It was thrilling to be back in school! Have I said I loved learning yet?!

At home, I found part-time jobs to help with bills and buying food. Plus, I liked the fact that working and going to school gave me less time at home to agitate my husband. He took great care of the kids, it seemed, so I was good there. He himself had a few jobs that would typically last a few weeks or maximum two months. He was a hard worker and bosses really liked him at first because he would go above and beyond tasks he was given. But he did not like authority or being questioned. Eventually when any of his bosses gave him direction, he would flip out so badly that he'd get fired. This happened more than once during our time together. So, it was better for him to stay home, I thought.

Chapter 10

OUR LAST CHRISTMAS

That year my parents wanted us to be home for Christmas.
I agreed. I didn't want to have another Christmas like the one we'd had
a year earlier. At that Christmas, we literally had nothing to eat in the
last week of December. We had budgeted enough money and groceries
to last until Christmas Day. I learned how to budget at Lindenview but
no amount of budgeting could've helped us that year. We couldn't get
any social assistance until the offices opened again a few days after New
Year's Day. I hope families relying on social assistance now don't have to
struggle the way many of us did then.

During that time, my ex-husband and I ate very little and our kids
seemed okay with just having instant noodles for a few days, they had no
choice. But we did save what we bought for Christmas dinner and actually made a nice big dinner, turkey and all. Other than that, Christmas
that year was bleak. The one bright light during that time was getting a
surprise delivery from Safeway.

One of my aunts from home, who gives presents to every single person
in her family and our extended family, had a fruit basket delivered.
Getting it felt like it saved us, like a cool drink of water on a very hot
day. It had bananas, berries, pears, and chocolates. I couldn't believe
how blessed we were, and our kids felt the joy from getting it too. And
as special as that was, I didn't want to risk having another Christmas
where my kids saw the stress of the season again.

This time, I wanted Christmas to be the best ever. I wanted to see
my big family and eat with everyone that came to share meals at my
parents' place. I wanted my children and husband to feel the love and
have fun we had at those dinners. It's the kind of Christmas I was
used to. We stayed at my parents' place. We went a week or so earlier

so my husband could work with my dad on building winter roads for our community.

We had a good visit and as expected our big family Christmas dinner was amazing. My grandfather was there, it would be the last time I spent the holidays with him. My parents' house was full of my aunts, uncles, cousins, and all their kids. A very full and loud fun Christmas. But after that day, when it was quiet at the house and no one was around, my husband got agitated about something. I don't think he realized my mom was in her room when he got angry at me. And we didn't realize it would be his last day there either.

He was getting impatient about something and he started to raise his voice at me, swearing. I felt very awkward because I had never heard a swear word spoken in my parents' home before this. He was cussing up a storm and stomping around the house loudly as he yelled and swore. His display was really stressing me out, though. This was nothing new to me and my kids, but I wanted him to stop so my mom wouldn't be worried. I even told him my mom was home. At first he paused but eventually said he didn't care if my mom was there. "I don't give a shit," he said. "Do you think I'm scared of your mom?" I was mortified. He kept this up until the door opened and thunder walked in. My dad. As soon as Dad walked in and slammed the door behind him, he asked me, "Where's your mom?"

"In the room," I said.

The door was shut and he shut it again after he walked in to find my mom. We all became quiet. Even my husband.

Just a minute or so later, my dad came back out of the room and walked straight up to my husband. We all froze not knowing what was going to happen. I took the kids into the bedroom and I could hear my dad talking to him. He told him to pack his things and that he was taking him to the airport. My husband said, "Well you need to pay me first, I'm not leaving here until you pay me." I looked out of the room and I saw my dad pull out his wallet and hand him a large wad of money. My husband came into the room we were in and packed his bag. He didn't even say goodbye to the kids or say anything to me. It's almost like he was super excited to be leaving.

He got his jacket and shoes on with the wad of cash my dad paid him in his pocket and left with my dad. Feeling awkward and not wanting to see my mom, my kids and I stayed in the room while my dad was gone. I didn't know what to say to my mom, I was embarrassed that she heard him yelling and swearing at me. About twenty minutes later my dad came storming back into the house without my husband. He came straight to the room and said, "Sheila you are an adult and I can't tell you what to do. But if I were you, I would never go back to that man."

The feelings that followed have stayed with me ever since that moment. I literally felt like there were handcuffs or chains breaking and falling off my wrists. I finally felt I could let my guard down and quit pretending that everything was okay. It was as if my parents were giving me permission to leave my husband. I was so relieved that I felt elated but heartbroken at the same time. As that happened, tears started flowing onto my face but I didn't let out a cry. I felt free, like I was just let out of jail or a desert! I went back to the room we were staying in and I lay down. I don't remember what else was said or what happened after that, I just remember that for the few days that followed I lay in bed crying. My mom took care of my kids and fed me. We didn't talk about what happened, but I knew they knew I was brokenhearted. I stayed in bed for three days straight, I was worried about my husband and I wasn't sure how long I was going to stay at my parents' place. But I felt free and after three days, I was done grieving. Done. I didn't worry about my husband anymore, I didn't feel like I had to go back to him, I felt like my kids and I would be okay. I felt a sense of hope that I hadn't felt in a long time. It felt good. It's hard to explain what happened or how it happened. The best way I've been able to describe my feeling from that time is like pulling an elastic. You pull the elastic and it has a lot of give. It can be stretched very far and very long. But if you keep stretching it and not let go, it eventually breaks and that's it. I feel like my heart and my emotions were the elastic, and once they broke, that was it. I was done with putting up with the abuse.

I believe the change of heart happened because my parents prayed relentlessly. I felt a sense of calm, a sense of optimism and even excitement for what the future could hold for my children and me. My parents were happy as well. They asked me to forget about Brandon and stay with them instead. I knew they were worried. If they ever knew how bad the abuse got with my husband and the dangers I was in as a teenager alone in Winnipeg, I think they would've been horrified and never let me out of their sight. But I told them I had to go back—I made a decision that I had to get on with my life with my children.

That was about four years after I had fled to Brandon, set my family up, gone to college, finished two diploma programs, and was getting ready for an internship in Winnipeg. One of the diplomas was for Business Accounting, the other for Rural Development (an economic, social, and environmental development program). We stayed at my parents' place for about two weeks longer. But I had to go back, I felt stronger and confident that the internship I had secured was going to be another good start for my kids and me.

We went back to Brandon and I started to get ready to move my kids and myself to Winnipeg for the Economic Development Officer internship I was offered by the Kitayan Community Futures Corporation. The internship called for almost all the skills I learned in the two programs I graduated from at Assiniboine Community College in Brandon: promoting entrepreneurship and promoting economic, social, and environmental development in the community. I was especially excited to get into First Nations to explore community development with them and get people excited about owning their own businesses. I felt very hopeful for the future of our people and for my family.

Before we moved to Winnipeg, my ex-husband tried to come back to the house in Brandon. I threatened to call the police every time he said he was coming. I was serious this time and he knew it. I was done taking any abuse from him. Him yelling and swearing the way he did while my mom was there was the last straw. And my dad telling me I didn't have to live like that was liberating and empowering.

It didn't mean he wouldn't keep trying though. When he ran out of money, he tried to take me on his guilt trip to let him come home. I stood my ground but one day he did come to the house, unannounced. It was a nice spring day and I was in the middle of packing boxes. It was mid-March just weeks before I moved to Winnipeg. The kids were super excited to see him. But the spell or whatever he had over me was gone. Instead, I saw a future without the abuse in my and my children's lives. I felt that if I stayed with him any longer there would always be drama in my life. Even for work or school, he would let his jealousy cause problems for me. One time as I headed to work at the nursing station in Bunibonibee, I had my hair in a ponytail and tried to take extra time to look professional. As I was leaving, my ex-husband stopped me at the door, looked at me and messed my hair up and told me, "There, go to work like that" as he shoved me out the door. He took my elastic, so I couldn't even put my hair up again! And he did things like that when I was going to school too, he didn't approve of me wearing anything revealing in any way.

When he showed up the last time in Brandon though, I didn't feel sorry for him, I didn't feel bad about being happy anymore and I didn't miss him as much as I used to. I was ready to move on. I certainly wasn't going to let him touch me in any way again.

This was getting frustrating for him and he got angry, of course. This time though, the outside door was open and a man walking by must've heard him and came into the house. This man was Reverend Henry Idonije. Rev. Idonije had a church just a few blocks from my house and we used to go for services there. His kids, including Israel Idonije, taught Sunday school to my kids. Yes, the professional National Football League (NFL) football player Israel Idonije taught my kids in Sunday School! Anyhow, Pastor Idonije walked in and said, "Pardon me. I heard all the yelling and I wanted to make sure everyone in here was okay." My ex-husband told him to get out and mind his own business. He tried to intimidate the large man, but Pastor Idonije wasn't intimidated in any way. I was embarrassed that he talked to the pastor like that, not only because he was a man of God, but he was a very nice, kind-hearted person who was always good to our family. His whole family was good to us, even to my ex.

Pastor Idonije stayed and kept offering to help in any way he could. My ex-husband softened his tone and told him that I was being difficult. Pastor told him in short, "The way I see it, is you have to let her go. Don't bother her, give her time and let her know you love her in other ways. If you do, you have a better chance at getting her back. Otherwise, you're going to lose her forever, and someone else will step in and enjoy your family."

I don't even know how or why that happened, but my husband did listen to Pastor Idonije and he left that day. That was really the end, and Pastor Idonije was right about all that. He did leave that day but when we finally moved to Winnipeg, my ex-husband didn't let up. He didn't heed the pastor's warning and kept showing up where I was, sometimes sweet, sometimes angry. But I was done and eventually had to get a restraining order against him to keep him away. A year and half after moving to Winnipeg, I met someone who stepped into our lives for seventeen years.

Chapter 11

NEW CHAPTER, NEW LIFE

The first few months of living in Winnipeg were challenging but fun. I had a job and I got the kids into school. In that first year the kids and I made new friends and I started to get pulled into politics. My boss at the time introduced me to his friends who were running a campaign for Phil Fontaine to become the National Chief of the Assembly of First Nations (AFN) in 1997. These friends were Jennifer and Darcy Wood, the same couple who would help me run my own campaigns years later. It was the first time I met them. They became some of my closest friends and still are.

When they and my old boss, Norman Wood, recruited me to work on Phil's campaign, Norman and my office was on the same floor as Phil's campaign headquarters for Manitoba. One day out of the blue, Norman came and asked me to follow him. "Come on, I want to introduce you to my friends next door. They're running a campaign," he said. I didn't really understand what that meant at the time, but I was happy to go meet his friends.

When I got in the room, Darcy and Norman greeted each other right away and he introduced me.

"Hello," Darcy said. "Nice to meet you, this is Jennifer," he said pointing at Jennifer who was on the phone laying down the law!

"I thought you said the office would be set up," she said sternly to someone on the phone. "There's no phone lines here, no fax machine, no copier. Nothing," she added. I couldn't help overhearing her while I was chit chatting with Darcy and Norman. Then Jennifer ended her phone call by slamming the receiver down and looked at us, pointed her left hand to me and said, "Hello. I'm Jennifer Wood. I'm behind everything of whatever he is," pointing at Darcy!

For a moment I wasn't sure how to take that, then we all burst out laughing about it. That was my introduction to the couple that basically, without any of us knowing, became my mentors. I was mistaken as their daughter many times since, and in a way I did feel like they were another set of parents for me since I met them. I feel very blessed about that.

But when I first started with them as a volunteer, I really didn't know what I was doing. I just did what I was asked to do. Get pens, make copies of posters, do phone calls, etc. During that time and at the election in Vancouver that year, I met the then-Assembly of First Nations National Chief, Ovide Mercredi. I also met the other candidates, including Wendy Grant-John, Bill Wilson (the father of Jody Wilson-Raybould) and others. My father used to talk about some of these people when he talked about politics, so I was super excited to meet them. Of course, they didn't know who I was, but I was grateful I got to meet them and my dad was too.

One of the first memorable moments from that time was being in Phil's campaign office. He came in to talk with the managers. "Hello, I'm Phil Fontaine," he said, reaching his hand out to me. He didn't remember that I had met him before. He'd been a guest speaker at ACC in Brandon about a year before that. One of my contacts had connected me to him and we arranged for him to come speak to our class about politics. He did great, of course, his presence created a buzz in our entire college.

I didn't want to waste his time trying to explain we had met before so I just said hello back. "Can you do me a favour?" he continued. "I have my car downstairs, here's the key and some money. Can you go to the Tall Grass Prairie bakery in Wolseley to get us all a dozen cinnamon buns?" I wasn't sure if he was serious at first, but I agreed. I took the keys and his twenty-dollar bill and went downstairs and found his car, a brand-new red Buick, and I got in and drove to the Tall Grass Prairie bakery. I had only met Phil once before and he didn't even remember who I was, but I was super nervous that he asked me. I didn't want to mess up the task. Which I did!

I was able to find my way to the bakery, which is impressive in itself, since there were no GPS maps on cellphones for me to follow at the time.

And I was new to the city. Anyhow, I got inside the bakery I asked for a dozen buns, and they packed them. They smelled and looked fantastic. I was ready to grab them and go but when I went to look for the $20 to pay for them, I could not find the money anywhere in my pocket. And I hadn't brought my purse or money to pay for it myself.

Oh, my goodness, I was horrified. I told the cashier that I had to run back to our office to get the money I didn't have. In a real panic, I rushed back to the office, retracing every step I made, including where I came down the stairs. The trip was fairly short, but it felt like an eternity.

And to my relief, I did find the stupid money. Ha! I found it sitting on the top of the third-floor stairs. I must've dropped it as soon as I left. I grabbed it with authority, rather angry at myself and wondered if I should run back to the bakery. In my mind, I thought yes, he asked me to and I have to. I ran back to the car, drove hastily back to get the buns, and rushed back to the office as fast as I could. I must've been gone for about a half hour and it should've only taken half of that time. I was hoping Phil didn't notice how long I was gone. But as soon as I saw him, I knew he was annoyed. And what else could I do but to try and make light of it.

I told him that I hit someone on the way but his car was okay. He wasn't happy, he didn't think that was funny! Everyone else laughed though when I said I was kidding. He left shortly after that. I think I was in his bad books for a while after that, but we all enjoyed the delicious gooey cinnamon buns after he left!

Another memorable moment from that AFN election in 1997 was being in Vancouver at the 'war room' a day before the actual voting day. Everyone else had left the campaign office for the night and I stayed behind to finish manually inputting numbers on spreadsheets hung on the walls of how voters—the Chiefs from across Canada—were saying they were voting leading up to the election. Other volunteers were calling as many of the over-630 Chiefs across Canada to see who they were thinking of voting for so Phil could talk to the ones who weren't supporting him. As I was working with my back turned to the door, I heard a man coming into the office asking, "Can I ask you a question?" It was Ovide Mercredi, the incumbent AFN National Chief. "I'm supposed to be at the same meeting with Phil and the Chiefs, but I forget where it is, can you tell me where the meeting is?" I must've looked as naïve as I was and I had no reason to not believe him, so I told him. "Thank you," he said. Looking very pleased.

The next morning, back in the 'war room' (we literally had a sign that said 'War Room' on the wall!) we were all busy working. Phil came in, clearly annoyed, and asked, "Who told Ovide where I was meeting with Chiefs last night?" I paused but sheepishly held my hand up, fessed up and told him it was me. He shook his head and didn't say anything else. I felt horrible. It was strike two for me during that campaign. Anyway, I hope Phil has gotten over those two incidents by now! Though he didn't remember who I was for several years, even after I met him several times and worked on his campaign.

In spite of my mishaps, our team was successful that year and it was exhilarating to be a part of it. Though, again, I didn't really know the impact of the elections then and even people in them. But I appreciated the experience and I stayed connected to many of the people I met. Three years after that election, the team I was involved with, including Jennifer and Darcy, was asked to run another man's campaign, Matthew Coon Come's. Matthew became the AFN National Chief from 2000 to 2003.

By this time, I was more aware of the politics and the importance of it all. Ever since I was very young, I've paid attention to politics and current affairs. Not a surprise because my father had always shown interest in politics—both Indigenous and mainstream. He had always paid attention to current affairs. News programs were pretty much all my parents allowed us to watch when I was young.

But it wasn't until I got involved in the campaigns that I really learned to appreciate how important all of that is. Important because I see the big role politics plays in our lives individually and collectively, whether we like to admit it or notice it or not. And that the few politicians involved are the ones making decisions on our behalf, whether we like to admit or notice it. I think it's important for all of us to be able to say who these politicians are, to make sure they know what you need to live in health, peace, and prosperity.

For example, when my family and I were struggling that one year to make ends meet during Christmas in Brandon, it would've been helpful for systems to be designed in a way that we could have had an easier time getting money for food we needed rather than going without until social assistance offices were open days after New Year's Day. As I said, at the time I was very good at creating and following a budget but there just weren't enough resources then to cover a few extra days. I think politicians and policy makers need to know—and many do know—the struggles young families go through like we did that year. So they may be able to make changes needed to make sure people don't go hungry in times like that.

When I lived on reserve it was a little easier because family would help each other and made sure we were all getting what we needed. Though in the bigger picture, reserves and anyone living there know what it's like to live in poverty. If it wasn't for the communal lifestyle of our Nations, we would be worse off and would have to go long periods of time without having what we need to keep families safe and healthy.

Unfortunately, colonization has changed drastically the ability for First Nations to be self-sufficient and largely took away the ability for families to live off the land, causing a myriad of problems for Indigenous Peoples now and since the Indian Act was imposed on the Original People.

I felt the imposition when my young family started living in an urban centre away from my extended family. We went without because living in the city is more of an individualistic culture. Though there are now more social services that help anyone struggling in our urban centres, when you're new to the city and don't have a nest of savings to rely on, you're really on your own. Again, all of this—who gets what, and who doesn't—is influenced by politics, politicians, and policy makers.

Getting involved in political campaigns also showed me what a sacrifice and challenge it can be for anyone to step up to run for a leadership position. It's deeply personal and anyone running never really runs alone because you need a team to help with all the work it takes to run in any election.

In the old ways, leaders were groomed, trained, and appointed mostly by women for their communities. Colonization has had its influence here too, changing the political systems that existed long before settlers ascended on this part of the world. Now we have leaders that have to compete for positions and not everyone who runs, runs for the right reasons. That's why I think it's important for more people to get involved in recruiting good candidates and helping them get in. Much like my father did when he helped Dorothy Grieves replace him as the chief of Bunibonibee in 1973. She is still the only female chief our community has had, however. The role of women in leadership has been deeply impacted by colonization, causing harm to Indigenous people in many ways. More about that later.

The competition during the AFN election in 2000 was fierce. Fierce as in intense, exhausting because of all the hard discussions that needed to be had and that were at times mean-spirited. In fact, each of the AFN elections I've been involved in seemed to be fierce, including the one I ran in as a candidate fifteen years later.

The people we had worked with just three years prior in 1997 on Phil Fontaine's campaign did not like seeing our team working on Matthew Coon Come's campaign. But it was what it was—Matthew's people asked us, and we decided to help. It was as simple as that. That year, Matthew Coon Come won and so did we. It was at those two elections that I feel my friends Jennifer and Darcy Wood stepped in to continue what my parents had been doing since I was very young—training me in Indigenous politics.

In those two AFN campaigns I was one of the people who'd do a variety of jobs like getting coffee for everyone, answering phone calls, managing other volunteers, and inputting numbers on electoral graphs. Being out of town and staying in a hotel was as glamorous as it got, because I was never able to afford to travel anywhere out of the province during that time. At the hotels I had to sleep on floors of other people's rooms because there wasn't always money for all volunteers to have their own rooms or beds during elections. I also remember not eating much because I didn't have a lot of money or time to eat. I didn't mind any of that though, I was in my glory just being there with everyone. I was in my groove! It was fun and I'm grateful for every moment of it.

Aside from campaigning during our first year in Winnipeg, I still had to do my job as the economic development officer intern for Kitayan Community Futures Corporation. My position and the office was funded by the federal government's Western Economic Diversification Canada department. Kitayan was one of more than a dozen organizations that served different sections of Manitoba. At Kitayan we served the region I'm from in the northeast part of the province, including Bunibonibee and Shamattawa First Nation.

My job included tasks that I had trained for at the college in Brandon— community development. And it involved travelling to communities promoting entrepreneurship for people living on reserves in northern Manitoba. I loved talking about the possibilities, but I realized that it was difficult for many on reserves to run or operate their own businesses. Difficult because most people didn't necessarily have what they needed for business startups for example.

The entrepreneurial spirit was alive and well though; it still is. We talked to people who know what Indigenous Peoples and communities need. They dream about independence; they strive to get back to self-sufficiency and are hard workers—much like Indigenous Peoples were before colonization. I recognized the spirit because my late father and my mother raised my siblings and I as entrepreneurs. They ran and operated a construction company for more than forty years. I saw them struggle many times, but they didn't let on that they were stressed. One common occurrence was seeing either my mom or my dad emptying their fridge and freezer for other parents who came to our door looking for a little bit of food to feed their families. My impression as a kid then was that my parents were well off and we always had enough to share what we had with others.

My parents got me excited about pursuing entrepreneurship and landing the internship as an economic development officer was a dream job for me. The new job and opportunities to meet hopeful people further woke my dreams of having a bright future for my children and me. During my conversations with would-be business owners, I got excited about being an entrepreneur as well. As a newly single parent and feeling a greater sense of independence, I decided to open my own business. I still believe promoting and striving to support the entrepreneurial spirit in First Nations is a valuable and necessary endeavor, a way to lift Indigenous Peoples out of poverty and harm's way.

While I was still an intern, I started working on my own business plan and market research to open a gift shop in Winnipeg. A good friend helped me at the time too. He is a great writer and researcher; I wouldn't have been able to get my little store off the ground without him and the support of a government program for business startups.

A year after moving to Winnipeg with my children, I left Kitayan and opened Indigenous Roots, a gift shop in the city's French Quarter, St. Boniface. I sold artwork, clothing, and jewellery from Indigenous artists from across Canada, Mexico, and Africa. My biggest sale was for thirty pieces of artwork that were used as gifts at a conference. It was a big sale that my children and I were able to celebrate because it sustained us for months. Coincidently, one of those art pieces ended up with my grandfather Wesley. He was presented with the framed painting as a gift for his years of service as an Elder with our Chiefs in Manitoba. It was a proud moment for me, especially when I saw his painting hung up at his house. He was very proud of it too, but I never explained to him that the piece came from my store. That wasn't important, I was just proud with him when he showed it to me.

One of the nicest moments we had at the shop was when I invited both of my children's classrooms to visit. They walked over from their school with their teachers and classmates. I had an Elder friend there to tell them a story and we fed them juice and bannock. I also made them little cards and a small gift that mentioned my kids and I owned the store. I don't know how significant that memory is to my children: I think they were still too young to really remember that time. But it was certainly a good day for me, and I got the impression everyone had a good time.

I loved owning my own business but it wasn't easy. One funny note though was on one of the first new days in my shop by myself. I was sitting there one moment wondering when the garbage was going to be taken out when I realized I had to empty it! The garbage would be emptied when I decided to do it. I had a good laugh at myself and I started to understand how much work it was to run a business. I ran the gift shop just blocks from where we lived near the Esplanade Riel bridge. During my market research, a few French people and other business owners literally told me I didn't belong there. "Go across the bridge to the English side if you don't speak French," one fellow businessperson said. I stayed and opened the shop anyway.

As things got tougher, I started thinking of ways to diversify. One of the artisans who brought goods in for consignment asked if she could buy into my shop. We decided to move to bigger, more expensive space together, so I gave my notice to the owner in St. Boniface that I wasn't signing another year-long lease. I packed up my goods and got ready to move. My friend and I found a place in Osborne Village, another popular business district in Winnipeg. However, as we were about to move, my friend called and said her financing fell through.

That meant I had to move to the new space by myself. I was already struggling to pay all the bills for the shop in St. Boniface as well as supporting my children and myself. I couldn't see how I could set up shop somewhere else by myself. So, after eighteen months or so of running Indigenous Roots, I decided to keep the shop packed, stored my products, and started looking for work.

The first job I found was as a driver for a fifteen-passenger van taking Indigenous patients from northern Manitoba to their doctors' appointments throughout Winnipeg. I got to meet people from home and other places. Most of the time we got to speak in Cree. It was a pleasant surprise for many of the patients and incredibly nice for me. Cree is my first language and I still think in Cree, especially when I really want to understand a concept. I constantly translate English into Cree in my head. Among the Indigenous languages on Turtle Island, Cree has the greatest number of speakers in Canada. Cree is only one of the several dialects spoken within the Algonquian language family. And Cree itself has several dialects as well. However, about half of all the seventy Indigenous languages in Canada that are spoken are in British Columbia.

· Elder D'arcy Linklater from the Nisichawayasichk Cree Nation told me during a visit with him that when we speak in public, we have to speak our mother tongue, our languages, first. "If Cree is your first language, you use that first when you talk to people, especially in public," Elder D'arcy said. "It honours our sovereignty as Indigenous people." I try to do that now in every public space I'm asked to speak in.

As in any cultural group, our Indigenous languages are an important part of what keeps us connected as people. Our languages shape how we think of the world around us and how we relate to others, the land, water, air, animals, food, life, etc. Our languages define us as Nations—without our languages we are not nations. The United Nations defines a nation as a community of people who have their own land and languages.

In an attempt to eliminate Indigenous Peoples from their own lands, our languages were banned from being spoken and cultural practices were prohibited through government laws and legislations, via the Indian Act and the creation of the Residential School System. Because of the resilience and strength of Indigenous Peoples, our cultures and languages have survived but continue to need protection and renewal.

For me, speaking Cree with the people I met when I was driving them to their appointments made me feel closer to my home and family. It was during that time I was reminded of another dream I'd had when I was a child. I wanted to become a medical physician. To explore the idea further, I decided to apply for a job as a Cree translator at the St. Boniface Hospital. I got the job and was able to walk the halls visiting patients and helping them communicate better with medical staff throughout the facility.

My dream to become a doctor didn't last long after I started at the hospital though. I saw how much time from their personal lives it took from doctors and nurses to do the necessary work. I admire that but as a single parent I had to think of my time with my children first. I wasn't able to commit to the time it would take to go to university, and I didn't have the resources to meet the needs of my family then either. And I found out I was actually squeamish during some medical procedures, so that didn't help!

Chapter 12

ENTER MY RAPPER HUSBAND

Just over a year after settling my children and myself in Winnipeg, as I was working on my business plan, I was scheduled for surgery on my right hip. I was glad, because the pain on the left side had subsided a bit from the first surgery but the right one was excruciating. When I woke up from the first surgery, I was surprised the surgeon had operated on the left one first because the right one seemed worse than the left one. Nevertheless, the doctor said it didn't matter because both were in bad shape. I just wanted the pain that had been there as long as I could remember to stop or lessen. As I got older the pain got worse and it got harder and harder to walk. I was more than happy to just get the other one done.

While recovering from the second surgery, my kids went to my mom and dad's in Bunibonibee for a few weeks while I stayed in the city. One weekend my dad, my sister Audrey, and a family friend and missionary Larry Russell from South Dakota, came to stay with me at my little apartment for a few days. Larry and my dad were like brothers, even though Larry was white and my dad, Cree. They knew each other since they were young men in their twenties. They were in town for other things and decided to go to a gospel tent meeting at a reserve close to Winnipeg, called Sagkeeng First Nation.

The three of them wanted me to go with them to the gospel meeting. I didn't really want to, but in the end of course I went. I didn't want to go mostly because I felt embarrassed that I had been separated from my husband. My dad, Larry, and Audrey didn't make me feel bad about being separated though. They had the best of intentions and I think they were trying to cheer me up. I must've been kind of depressing to talk to during that time. Ha!

In my own head though, I felt church folk wouldn't want to see me or know me after leaving my husband. In fact, I retreated from almost everyone I knew because of that. I had one new friend who helped me unintentionally by distracting me from my new reality. He helped me with my business plan and became one of my only friends for almost a whole year. And I was perfectly fine with that.

But when my visitors came and pestered me to go with them, I saw it as a chance to get out of town for a few hours and be with them. We went for supper first and headed out of town. It was a fun little trip with plenty of laughs. My dad and Larry were funny together. When we got there, there were only about twenty people in the big white top tent—not the packed tent I was used to seeing at gospel meetings as a kid. I was pleasantly surprised about that. It was basically our little group, the pastor and his family and a few others, as well as these guys who clearly weren't from Sagkeeng, an Ojibway First Nation north of Winnipeg. These guys, a pastor from a Winnipeg children's church, Pastor Sumter, and four of his parishioners were the only Black people there. They certainly got my attention. Little did I know one of them would be my life partner for almost two decades

They were fairly quiet and so were my sister and I. But in my dad's usual fashion, he went up to speak and invited, actually 'voluntold,' my sister and me to get up and talk in front of everyone. They call it testifying in the church world. We did. Standing there with my crutches, still recovering from my latest surgery, I talked about how grateful I was to God for a speedy recovery from my two surgeries. My parents have always taught us to give thanks to God for everything when we had the opportunity. "I just want to say how happy I am that God saw me through my last surgery," I said. "God is good and my pain is nowhere near what it used to be," I ended. Then my sister and I sang a song in Cree! I couldn't believe that actually happened as I sat down. Singing away in front of these cool guys sitting in the front row! They made me nervous but excited.

At the end of the service, we all stuck around to have sandwiches and tea. Pastor Sumter and one of the guys came over and introduced themselves to us. The one guy, Carlos, asked my sister if she only knew three chords on the guitar! We laughed. I don't think he was trying to be funny, but it made us chuckle anyway. I asked him if any of them rapped. Carlos said, "Rob does." He turned around to look for Rob, but he wasn't there. I didn't know which one Rob was until he came back over to where we were all standing. I asked him if he could 'rap' for me. He said, "No. I'm just getting a sandwich!" That was my first conversation with my future husband, Robert (Rob) Wilson. Carlos said, "Don't worry about him, he's shy."

Before we all left the guys invited us to visit their children's church and we said we might show up one day. "Come by and meet the kids," Carlos said, "You'd love them, and they'll love you," he added. My sister replied, "Yes okay, we will. We'll surprise you one day." Audrey was better at flirting then I was! Rob told me later that he was interested in meeting us too but didn't want to seem like he was trying to pick up chicks at a church service. He says as they drove home that night, he prayed to God that he'd meet a girl like me someday and marry her! But he played it pretty cool that night.

Two weeks or so after this first meeting, my sister and I saw their big noticeable bus parked outside the church. The 'Children's Mission,' was located right in the heart of Winnipeg's North End. I hobbled into the church, still using crutches. Once inside, we saw dozens of young children running around, having fun. Some were colouring at a table as Rob was playing the drums on a stage. As soon as he saw us, he stopped playing and came over to talk to us. Carlos came over too, inviting us to stay awhile.

"Come sit down, we have some food. Do you want any juice or tea?" he asked.

"No, we are on our way to eat somewhere," Audrey replied.

We were only there for a few minutes. Long enough to have a quick visit and long enough for Rob to ask us for our phone numbers. "We are having a birthday party for one of our friends tonight, do you girls want to come?" Rob asked us.

Audrey said, "maybe."

"Well give me your numbers and I'll call you about it later."

Audrey gave him our numbers and I didn't oppose.

As we left the Children's Church an old dusty truck pulled up and out jumped one of the other guys we met at the tent meeting in Sagkeeng, Wes. He was one of those people who was naturally funny all the time. As my sister and I walked toward our car, he said in a panic "Wait, wait let me get your numbers."

Rob, who was standing on the steps with Carlos and some of the kids yelled out, "Come on man, we have their numbers already."

He said, "Okay but I want the one with the crutches."

We all had another good laugh.

That same evening Rob called to invite us to a birthday party at his house. I didn't know what to expect because I wasn't used to going to any social events, so I was a bit nervous. Drunk people actually scared me! As a child I remember only two times I saw and heard a drunk person. One was my late dad's uncle in Pimicikamak, my dad's home reserve. When this uncle got drunk, he would sometimes come to the house we were staying in and would talk loudly and cry a lot. I had never seen or heard an adult cry like that before, but he did. I was a small child when I saw that, and I didn't know that a few years earlier, during the Sixties Scoop, my uncle had come home from work from his job at the Canadian National Railway, and found all of his ten children taken away. All but one of his children were taken at the same time. One of the boys stayed with his mother. His other children were scattered all over Manitoba and the United States. About twenty thousand children were taken this way by child welfare officials from the 1950s to the 1980s. Many of the children were displayed in newspapers as possessions for white people to obtain. My cousins from this era still struggle with the ramifications of their experiences. My uncle died without ever regaining custody of his children.

The Sixties Scoop was similar to the Residential School era, where children were taken away or sent away from their families and home communities. The government wanted to "Kill the Indian in the Child" and so sent Indigenous children to boarding schools away from their families and communities. The children were subjected to all forms of abuse and attempted genocide under the guise of education. The schools operated for about 160 years and about 150,000 children attended. Some never made it home, dying at the schools and many were buried in unmarked graves near the schools instead of their bodies being returned to their families. In 2008, the work of the Truth and Reconciliation Commission of Canada (TRC) began gathering stories of survivors and thrivers from that era. It issued 94 Calls to Action, where it was hoped that Canada and Canadians would begin to move toward Reconciliation with the Original People of Canada.

While writing this book, the first of hundreds of unmarked graves were discovered at the former Kamloops Residential School. The TRC report had predicted there were many bodies at former sites that hadn't been discovered, yet the Canadian media reported the discoveries and subsequent discoveries as unexpected. But families and former students weren't surprised. In fact, many told stories of deaths and burials they witnessed at the schools long before the proof was splashed all over the media.

The second person I remember being drunk had been in a residential school. She too was crying, angry, and she barged into our house and grabbed a knife from one of the kitchen drawers. My mom and one of my sisters were home. My mom told us to hide, and we could hear my mom trying to get the knife out of the woman's hands. There was a lot of commotion then it stopped as my mom successfully got her out of the house. These two incidents stuck with me throughout my childhood, and I associated drunks and drinking with fear and pain.

But I thought that if Rob and his friends went to church then they probably wouldn't serve alcohol. I was wrong. The first surprise was pulling up to Rob's apartment. It was an upstairs suite of an old building near the corner of Selkirk Avenue and Main Street, one of the poorest neighbourhoods in the city. I was used to being in Winnipeg's North End because I lived just a few blocks from where I had lived in high school as a billeted student with my ex-mother-in-law. The same place I was staying at when I met my first husband. Still, Rob's apartment seemed cold and dark as we pulled up. We gave it a chance anyway.

Standing at the door waiting for someone to answer our knock, Audrey and I nervously looked at each other wondering what we got ourselves into. As the door swung open, there was Rob, cigarette in hand and a huge Budweiser poster of a woman in a bikini behind him. A whiff of marijuana billowing out toward us, Rob invited us in. We looked at each other, still worried. Rob was there with most of the friends he was with when we first met them. They were very nice and happy to see us again, and we were happy to see them.

"Come in, come. Have a seat, do you want any beer, do you need a smoke?" asked one of Rob's friends.

"It's okay," answered Audrey.

I didn't say much, I was nervous and excited to meet everyone though. Sensing we were a little nervous, Rob had us sit in the living room away from all the booze, smokes, and friends. He sat with us and showed us pictures in his photo album. He showed us pictures of his mom, his sister, and his son. He did his best to make us comfortable. But we didn't stay long. Especially as it seemed to get louder, I was really nervous. Audrey must've sensed this and announced we had to, "Go now."

After we left, it felt to me that we wouldn't see the guys again. I felt too square for them. But my sister suggested we go back and invite Rob for a coffee run. We both agreed he seemed genuinely sweet. We went back and called him from a payphone, because no one really had cell phones at the time. Audrey made me ask.

"Do you want to come for coffee with us?" I said to Rob.

"Hang on," he said, and he made us wait a few minutes before he agreed to come.

"We'll come back and pick you up," I said.

Turns out he was asking one of his friends if he should go, saying he was nervous. He said his friend encouraged him to come, saying, "You never know what may happen from this." He came and we went for a drive and talked over coffee at a restaurant.

When we dropped him back off, he got out, said goodnight, and turned to walk away. But in a flash, he turned back around and asked, "Can I call you later?" Kind of surprised, I said, "yes." Surprised because I thought he thought I was too quiet. I didn't talk much at any point. Audrey was braver and again better at flirting than I was, still is! But thanks to her, I met Rob and after that night, Rob and I began talking every day. And it didn't take long for us to figure out that we wanted to get to know each other more.

A week after we met again, my sister and I flew to Vancouver for a quick trip. Rob and I talked every chance we got. I bought him some gifts and soon I was only thinking about him! I'm sure my sister was annoyed. Soon after we got back to Winnipeg my sister left to go back home to Bunibonibee and my new friend and I started visiting more. Eventually, when my kids came home, I introduced them to Rob. They were of course not sure about him because he wasn't their dad. But Rob was really good to them and they liked him right away, especially when he'd include them in everything we did.

At the same time, we started going to the Children's Mission with him and we became really close friends with everyone there. It was there that I got to see my new boyfriend rapping for the first time. I didn't know much about the genre or lifestyle before that, but Rob started introducing me to it all and I became a fan.

I wanted to help him do more of what he was good at. I asked him what would help, he said "recording an album." Coincidently, one of my friends I met when I first moved to Winnipeg as a teen had a recording studio. I asked him if he would record an album for Rob. He did it for $600. It was a cassette tape, which was the most modern way to listen to and share music at the time. My friend Doug and his wife Tracy invited us to stay at their place in Peguis, Manitoba while Rob and Doug recorded songs for a couple of days. After they finished on the last evening, all of us stayed up all night shrink-wrapping each cassette tape. I designed the cover with clip art and filled in sections with the credits Rob wanted. It was fun to see it all come together and see Rob so happy.

We made five hundred cassettes and started selling them to our friends and family. Rob also started playing at more churches and cafes, and soon we sold out of the first batch of tapes. One of them even ended up in Albuquerque, New Mexico with a music producer named Tom Bee. Turns out the music producer was very involved in the Grammys every year and he had several artists he helped become Grammy Music Award nominees and winners.

None of this meant anything to me at the time because I didn't know what the Grammys were, and I didn't follow celebrities then either. But later on, we knew what the American awards were because Tom asked

Rob and his friends to make another album on compact disc. Tom asked his colleagues at Sunshine Records, a Winnipeg record label, to work with them. Coincidently, Sunshine Records was right next door to where Rob was living when I first met him, on Selkirk Avenue. They recorded the album and began playing in more shows, making a bit more money.

Chapter 13

ANOTHER TRANSITION

This was also the time I was still trying to get away from my ex-husband who did not like the fact that I met someone else. He did not like Rob hanging out with the kids and me. He harassed me by phone, threatened us, came to places my kids, Rob, and I were and challenged my boyfriend to fights. Rob never engaged him, even when he walked into a place we were at and swore right in his face. Rob was fine and not afraid for himself, but I was afraid for my kids. I didn't want them to be hurt further by their dad's behaviour. It took a toll on all of us when my ex became relentless again.

There were times I heard my children's father tell our kids that I was a horrible person. He told my kids I was sleeping around and letting other men put their penis in me. Our children were only eight and six at the time. I believe my children's father was trying to turn our children against me and hurt me. Not so much hurt our children, but more about hurting me and any man I was hanging out with. He would say this to them in front of me, while pointing at me. My children were of course horrified by him speaking that way to them.

One time, my ex came over to my and my children's little apartment, with his new girlfriend parked outside, trying to have sex with me. He was dropping off our kids and shoved me into a room when he got inside.

"Come on, I want to talk to you," he said.

"No," I replied, pushing him back.

He pulled me up and over into the room anyway. "You think you're too good for me now? You know, no one really wants you because you have two kids, right?" he said while fondling me.

He kept trying to take my clothes off and I fought back. I wasn't letting him do what he wanted. I don't think the kids noticed us going into the room at first. When they did they started pounding on the door to get in the room. He was almost successful in getting his way with me, but he stopped and let the kids in. But not before he said, "I don't want you anyway. You're ugly. You should see my new girlfriend, she's much better looking than you'll ever be," he said with a laugh. It wasn't the first time he pinned me down, trying to do what he wanted. He did that even while we were married several times. It's like he got a thrill from doing that. This time, however, he stopped, got up and mocked me instead. He left shortly after and said bye to the kids.

It wasn't until I had a restraining order in place that he slowed down in harassing us. But it wasn't easy to get the order. The magistrate didn't seem to believe how scared I was of my ex-husband. It felt like she was dismissing me. When I thought about leaving the place without a protection order, I got really scared. I didn't know what my next option would be. While I was in the shelters, I was taught about the protection orders and told where to apply for one. But I didn't know it was that hard to get until I sat there and sensed the magistrate starting to end our conversation.

"I don't think you are in danger; it sounds like a bad break up, but you'll be okay. If we put an order against him, we could ruin his reputation," she said.

"Ruin his reputation?" I thought. "What about our lives, what if he hurts us or kills us?" That's when I felt I had to get real and give the woman a real example, I didn't think it had to get to that point.

She started putting her papers away and I felt like she was telling me the conversation was over. I panicked in my head and started talking again. I cried a little as I started talking again. That's when she really started listening to me. Maybe she was giving the hint that I wasn't telling her enough information or that I wasn't telling her the right information for her to give me a protection order. I got the message and I started sobbing.

"My ex called me just a few days ago asking if I heard about a shooting in the city where a man was shot point blank in his head as he sat in a restaurant," I told her. "He told me that, laughed and hung up," I added. "He didn't directly threaten to shoot me or Rob, but he was alluding to the fact that anything like that could happen to anybody like that," I said. "Including me and the kids," I concluded, wiping my eyes.

I don't know at what point she agreed that I needed a protection order but finally she said I would be getting one. I'm not sure where any of us would be without it.

Seven months after we met, Rob proposed to me. He had joked about getting married before, but this time was different. He got down on one knee on my birthday in 1999, the same day I had a grand opening of my gift shop. It was a busy day for me, I had guests coming to join me and I was working furiously to make the shop look nice. Rob was helping me but then just before my guests started arriving, he stopped me, knelt down and asked me to marry him. I wasn't sure at that time I wanted to get married again but it was such a hectic day that I just said yes to get on with the day. I was also a little resentful that he asked me on my special day, my store's grand opening. It's almost as if he didn't want to be overlooked, he needed to make his presence known with me. Of course, I knew he was there, and I was grateful he was. But I do wish he had waited for another special day to ask me. Getting the shop to opening day was special enough, I thought.

But I also agreed because I was feeling guilty again for allowing him to stay at my place so much, while not being married to him. I knew my parents didn't approve of me 'living in sin' and I didn't want to disappoint them any further than I already had. I loved Rob and we got along very well. Eight months after he proposed we got married, just before Y2K, on December 17th, 1999. I don't regret marrying him, I felt I needed a father figure for my children and he got along great with them. And Rob was very loving as well, so it made sense to me to marry him, even though I felt I wasn't ready to marry so soon after divorcing my ex.

We got married on a cold winter evening. Rob rented a tuxedo and my son wore the tux I got him for his Christmas concert that year—Sonny had played Harry Belafonte that year. Trisha and I bought our dresses at a little Asian dress shop. The dresses were very pretty and clearly economical! We didn't spend a lot of money for the entire day. Our biggest purchases were the clothes. My sisters bought the decorations and decorated the recreation hall of the church we had the wedding in.

They also took pictures for us. On the day of the nuptials, it took us all only about an hour to get ready.

About thirty people joined us at the wedding. Half of them were there thinking they were coming to a regular church service that night. The other half was my family and a few friends. The ceremony was short, and my son wanted to be baptized so my dad baptized him the same night. After the ceremonies we all went to the back hall of the church and had a potluck-style meal that was mostly prepared by my mom and a multi-level cake baked by a friend. At the reception there was no music, no dancing. In fact, it felt like we were just at an after-church meal, except we were dressed a little more fancy than usual. We were happy though and everyone seemed to be having a good time. At the end of the night, we checked in to a hotel that Dad paid for as a wedding present to us. Then we headed off to a life some were sure would quickly end in disaster.

Chapter 14

NEW LIFE

After we started our new life together, Rob and I started talking more about our dreams and aspirations. I had never talked about any of that with my ex-husband, seeing someone excited about the future was all new to me. I also noticed how much Rob, who went by the moniker 'Fresh I.E.,' loved creating music. In my limited opinion, he was a great rapper and producer. I wanted to support his dreams of recording albums and performing live in front of big crowds.

He supported my dream of telling stories on TV, radio or in print. It wasn't until I met Rob that I remembered that I wanted to be a journalist. I always watched the news and loved current affairs. He introduced me to the idea of what a celebrity was, as he was becoming one. Just over a year after we met, I found a radio course I wanted to take. It seemed like the best option for me at the time, not really knowing what I needed to take to get into reporting on TV. As soon as I started taking classes, I felt awakened. I was excited about life even more because I remembered that as a kid I'd told my mom I wanted to be a reporter like Sandra Lewis, a former CBC news anchor.

"Write a letter to her," Mom said at the time.

"What will I say," I remember asking Mom.

"Ask her about her job and things like her earrings," she said. "Just talk to her."

I never did get the nerve to write a letter to Sandra, but I kept admiring news people, hoping someday I'd be one.

I told Rob stories like that, and he would say, "Someday you are going to be on CBC." I felt safe enough to dream big and not be ridiculed, the way my ex did when I talked about ideas or hopes I had. Rob obviously felt safe in telling me his hopes as well as we both started to dream out loud to each other.

None of our dreams really felt achievable though, at least not to me. It was the events of 9/11 in New York in 2001 that really galvanized our dreams. Getting ready one morning for school, I was stopped in my tracks at the sight of a plane crashing into one of the Twin Towers in New York. I changed the channel to see if any of the Canadian news networks were covering the crash. Seeing it on almost every channel I quickly realized how serious the event was. Everywhere you turned you saw images of the terrorist attack on America, smoke billowing from the Twin Towers into all of our lives, just before they collapsed.

Like most people I thought it was just a horrible accident at first, but that didn't make it any less polarizing. Rob was at work at a gas station, I always made sure he was working to help pay the bills! When another plane hit the second Twin Tower, I called Rob to ask if he was watching what was happening. He was.

"Babe, are you seeing what's going on in New York," I asked him.

"Yup," he said. "It's messed up. The world is going crazy."

The kids were already in school but even they couldn't escape hearing about the event heard around the world. Their teachers tuned in in their classrooms to watch with all of the students.

As I tried to rush out of the house to get to class myself, I couldn't. I stayed glued to the TV well until after both towers collapsed. The whole day became all about 9/11. When I eventually got to class, we were told to go back home and continue watching the events unfold on TV. We were to watch and bring our thoughts the next day. And as we all saw the catastrophe change the entire world, change came to our little world.

When we all got home, still reflecting on the day, Rob told us he had decided right there that he was going to pursue music full time. I had already started pursuing my dream of becoming a journalist. That day I also felt stronger than ever that I was on the right path—I wanted to be a storyteller. We all talked about how scary the images from New York were as Rob and I tried our best to explain what was going on. Not really understanding ourselves, then, what a terrorist was. We all quickly learned though, and I think the event gave Rob and I the notion to get serious with our dreams. To pursue them with purpose. Which we did.

The next day Rob quit his job as a gas jockey and hunkered down in front of the beat machine his grandmother had bought for him out of the blue one day. She told him she wanted him to pursue his dreams of making music. For the next year he sat in front of the MC-303 beatmaker, teaching himself to make music. Before that he had never taken a music lesson or class, he just went off the sounds from his favourite albums. Eventually he made his own beats to rap to.

Next came the need for a microphone, a computer to record onto, speakers, and other hardware needed to record the music. I remember everything costing a lot of money. Money we didn't really have in the first place. I was just a student at the time. Still, day after day, night after night, Rob sat there in our living room learning to make music.

We continued to struggle financially, neither of us bringing home much money. I headed off to school and he'd do an odd little appearance here and there performing the music he was making but not getting paid much. There were many, many moments we doubted each other and got at each other's throats. Especially when we literally ran out of money. More than once he would say in frustration, "Grow up, stop going to school and get a job! You've had enough time to go to school."

I would reply in a huff and say, "You're wasting your time in trying to make music, go back to work, you can't promise your music is going to get you anywhere."

However, no matter how high the stress levels got or how long we had to go without money, neither of us was willing to stop pursuing our dreams.

That following summer, in 2002, we decided to send our kids to visit my mom and dad's, up North. Partly to give them a break from Winnipeg but mostly because we had little to no money at times to buy enough groceries for all of us. I remember crying a few times as I headed to school, complaining to myself, "I can't even buy a cup of coffee." What made that feeling worse was going to school in a mall, seeing all the stuff and food I couldn't buy! But I survived! Thanks in large part to a part time job I got at Orange Julius in the same mall I was taking classes in. During the day I went to class and on most evenings, I'd be in the food court serving up smoothies and hot dogs. I didn't mind at all; it was nice to make a little bit of money.

One of the lowest times though was when I did have some money but not enough to buy all the groceries we needed. To help, I compromised and made a stop at a dollar store on my way home to buy a small package of ground coffee. I was so happy thinking I was going to make a good cup of joe for Rob and myself in the morning. It smelled normal but it was the only similarity to a decent cup of coffee it had. We tried to drink it but we couldn't stomach the taste past one sip. It was horrible, so bad we had to laugh about it. Yuck! It was as if the coffee had salt in it or very bad water. Thankfully, friends of ours from out of town came to stay with us throughout the summer and bought us groceries here and there. It was a hard year, but we managed to keep ourselves motivated.

When I completed my courses at the Academy of Broadcasting Corp, I went to audition at Native Communications Inc. (NCI FM) in Winnipeg, the Indigenous radio station that broadcasts throughout Manitoba. They needed a Cree/English announcer and I needed the work. After the audition, the manager told me he'd try me out for three days. I stayed for three years.

The first day was nerve-wracking. The manager showed me the basics of the studio and told me to sit and get comfortable with using the control board and microphone. The closest I was to a microphone before that was singing in church. But this was very different. This was me finding myself in a professional studio, wondering what I had done! Questioning myself, wondering if I could even talk in front of the microphone. It felt like a time when I was kid and found myself in some quicksand until my dad had to come pull me out! But Dad wasn't around me at this moment, so I had to figure things out myself.

As I took my place in front of the microphone; I started shaking because I wasn't sure I could do what I had been so sure I could do during the interview—be on radio or TV. As I sat trembling, a seasoned announcer came in and showed me which buttons to push and which sliders to slide to record my first on-air appearance as a Cree personality. After showing me a few times how to use the equipment, the other announcer left the room, encouraging me to practice. Looking at the microphone again and seeing my hands trembling, I doubted myself. I prayed under my breath, "God, if this is really what you want me to do then you have to help me. I don't know if I can do this."

I opened my eyes, took a deep breath, turned the music and microphone on and started talking with no feeling of nervousness in my body whatsoever. In fact, since I prayed that little prayer, I haven't felt nervous or scared sitting in front of a microphone or camera since. At least not enough to doubt myself. Strange but true. And while being a radio DJ was fun and exciting, I knew I needed to keep going to pursue journalism. Being on radio as an announcer was a great start though.

Back at home, Rob finished off his first commercial album he called *Red Letterz*. It became his first solo project. In the songs he spoke about emotions he felt as a child who was forced to grow up fast. Once he was done recording, he and Tom Bee reconnected. Rob shared the solo project with him, Tom asked if he could share it with a few music executives he knew. Rob agreed, not knowing it would lead us to being at the Grammy Award show in Los Angeles just months later in February 2003.

Chapter 15

THE GRAMMYS

Tom Bee, a Native American record label owner from Albuquerque, New Mexico, asked Rob if he could submit *Red Letterz* to the Grammy Awards for consideration. Neither of us really understood what that meant right away, but it became really exciting when Tom called with frequent updates of how the record was moving up the ranks in the weeks that followed. Again, I didn't fully realize then that it was a tremendous honour for artists just to be nominated for these music awards.

Tom submitted the album in the Rock Gospel category in the fall of 2002. Once he did, he'd call and say, "the album made it into the next round." The album started off as one of over a thousand submissions. Then it was in the top one hundred, the top fifty, the top ten and finally in the top five! Top five meant he was an official Grammy Award nominee.

The moment we found out was one evening in December 2002. Rob had just picked me up from NCI where I just finished my shift on the radio. He got a call on his cell from a friend who simply asked, "So when do you want to sign the management contract?"

Rob asked, "What are you talking about?"

"You didn't hear?" the friend asked.

"Hear what?"

"Dude, you've been nominated for the Grammy Awards," he said with a chuckle.

We both sat in the car stunned. It was like a train had hit us. The feeling was amazing. I felt a huge sense of relief and joy, it was almost like we were being rewarded for all the sacrifices we made.

"Stop playing around," Rob said with a nervous smirk. But the friend assured us he was serious. We couldn't believe it. It wasn't until we read the nomination list on the Grammy website for ourselves that we actually believed it. *Red Letterz*, listed among the top five in its category. It was overwhelming, exciting, and just so surprising. Nothing that big had ever happened in either of our lives before. My husband made history and became the first Canadian rapper to ever be nominated for a Grammy Award. Even before Drake, Rob was nominated for the prestigious American music award. As soon as we got home, there were calls from several local journalists wanting to speak to Rob about the nod. We were shocked, we had no idea how they found our numbers! With the nomination we began dreaming about going to the actual award show in Los Angeles.

The weeks that followed we got even more excited but also stressed again. We still didn't have much money, no disposable income at least. And certainly no money to take us to Los Angeles for the award show. Friends of ours started helping us raise funds and offered the air miles from their credit cards to get us there. We also threw a fundraising party to celebrate the nomination and made enough money to pay for our hotel rooms in L.A. The whole experience was surreal. With help from friends, we were able to get everything we needed to go to music's biggest night. A white suit for Rob, a custom-made dress for me by a designer out of Calgary, Alberta and all the accessories we needed to complete our looks! The lead up to the event became more intense and elaborate than even our wedding.

What added to the intensity was all the media attention Rob was suddenly attracting. Every local reporter and all the national news shows wanted to hear his story. They were as amazed as we were that someone from Winnipeg's North End was being nominated for a Grammy. Some dug around trying to find out if Rob had a criminal past. Many were wondering if he was telling the truth about his past. One reporter even suggested he was lying about his past and that we actually had 'deep pockets.' Deep enough that we paid our way to a nomination. We were flabbergasted at the thought, knowing we had barely scraped up enough money to buy dollar-store coffee just months before.

Before we jetted off to Los Angeles, we went to Toronto, Ontario so Rob could appear on the *Mike Bullard Show*, a Canadian late-night talk show. That in itself was a good experience. We had so much fun being treated like celebrities and friends of ours who helped plan the trip came with us to Toronto and played live music on the show. Having them there certainly made it more exciting. Sadly though, we didn't have enough money to take our children with us. But we were in constant contact with them and I gave them a play-by-play of all the events we went to.

When we finally arrived in Los Angeles, we were only there for five days. But it was incredibly exciting. Thankfully, most of the trip was chronicled by a Winnipeg CTV news crew. The crew followed us everywhere and took us to all the usual touristy spots in Hollywood. The crew eventually turned the footage into a half-hour special they aired weeks after the trip. *ET Canada* was in L.A. too and interviewed Rob during one of our limousine rides. Like I say, it was all too surreal.

Tom Bee was right by our side at the Grammys too, showing us the ropes. He took us to pre-Grammy parties and events. It seemed like Tom knew everyone, and everyone knew him. He knew where we needed to go to get, for example, the Grammy medal each nominated artist was given. He knew where we needed to go to collect that, and he took us to where Rob was to get his official Grammy photo. Plus all the dinners in between all the events we got to go to were mind blowing. All kinds of food that we'd only seen on TV, elaborate parties that we were never a part of before. Just amazing. We were wide-eyed throughout, I'm sure.

We met many great people and what surprised us the most was how all the events we went to had celebrity after celebrity. Fans were not really in the mix other than the ones who camped outside venues where parties were being held. Most of the people were industry people and big-name stars rubbing shoulders with each other talking normally to each other like nothing out of the ordinary was going on. Asking each other how their families were, asking about directions to certain places, or simple hellos and good laughs. And then there was us trying to take it all in. We were so overwhelmed with the whole trip we hardly ate. I think we only ate once a day and went back to our hotel room exhausted every night.

The day and night of the Grammy was the best. We were in the same circles as rapper Jay-Z, legendary singer Shirley Caesar, and Andre 3000. We were sitting behind former American Idol singer Ruben Studdard, and boxer Evander Holyfield was not too far away eating an ice cream!

Again, surreal. I remember being at the show and being cold. Partly because I was shaking with excitement, but it was also cold in the Staples Centre. The show that year was opened by Beyoncé and Prince. Just before the show started, we saw them mingling around near where we were sitting. Rob and I just kind of huddled together. I think we were in shock just being there. We only went to about three pre- and post- parties, there were plenty to choose from. The one party we did go to got a little crazy. I was wearing a short leather skirt and Rob was wearing a black suit. Both of us were getting hit on and we didn't know how to handle it! It's kind of funny to think about it now, we must've looked like scared little teenagers. Tom was having a few laughs. We did later on.

That year, the carpet was green because it was sponsored by Heineken Breweries, but we didn't get to walk on it because we took the time out to meet the CTV crew in between the early awards show and the televised show. Rob's category was in the early show. He didn't win, but it didn't matter at the time. Being there was more than enough excitement for us. One of the very last things he told the CTV crew after we came out of the first awards show was "I'll be back, I already have the title of the next album: *Truth is Fallin in the Streetz*."

He was right. Two years after the first nomination, his next commercial release, *Truth is Fallin in the Streetz* was submitted once again by Tom Bee. Then Rob "Fresh I.E." Wilson became a two-time Grammy Award-nominated rapper. And once again, like the first year, we lost to Audio Adrenaline! But what was really great about the second trip was being able to take the kids with us to Los Angeles. It became a family trip. We raised money again, found a few sponsors to help with clothing and headed to Tinseltown.

During our first trip we met a couple at one of the Grammy parties. The woman volunteered to help me get ready for the show. At that time, she offered to do my hair and make-up. She came and she made the experience of being there even better for me. On our way to the second trip to the Grammys we called the couple up again and they met us at our hotel when we got there. The woman again, out of sheer kindness, took our kids, who were now teens, on a tour of Hollywood. The Spanish woman with her beautiful accent said, "Don't worry, I'll show them the best spots." She did. Our kids came back that evening talking about all the little cool places they went to in Hollywood. They saw spots where celebrities hung out or lived and went to places like the Hollywood Walk of Fame. I brought her a few gifts from home to thank her for her kindness.

While she helped to entertain our young teens, Rob and I did all the usual Grammy-related appearances. Getting his second nominee medal, getting his portrait done, it was just as exciting as the first time. During the Grammy Award show itself, the media and talk shows were more interested in how Justin Timberlake and Janet Jackson would act after the 'wardrobe malfunction' that had happened during their performance at the Super Bowl a week earlier. They wanted to see if anything similar would happen at Timberlake's performance for the Grammys. It didn't. The second time we were there, we took more time to look around at the pre and post parties. At one of the official Grammy after parties, we sat at the same table as Joe Jackson, the famous/infamous father of the Jacksons. Rob said hi to him.

"How you doin' son?" he asked Rob.

"I'm good, I'm good" he answered. "I love your jacket and hat," Rob added.

Joe was wearing a jean jacket with the face of Richard Pryor on it, designed with sequins, and a matching baseball-type hat. "Thank you," he said.

Pryor had passed away shortly before that time.

Will.i.am from the Black-Eyed Peas was at the same party and entertained us all, while people on stilts walked around all of us overhead. At first the tall sticks were dormant but after a while it was clear that the sticks with vines all around them were stilts and people were on there slowly moving around and over us. It was wild, yet mild I'm sure compared to other people's experiences there.

Overall, the second trip to the Grammys was more memorable because we got to see the excitement and thrill on our children's faces as they experienced the Grammys for the first time. They got dressed up too and got to see some of Hollywood's biggest celebrities with us. It was so much fun and all four of us learned so much together. We learned we could dare to dream and set high goals for ourselves. We grew closer to each other and realized anything was possible.

The second trip was chronicled this time too, by an independent film crew. They too followed our every move and got to share some special moments with us. They shot many hours of footage from the trip and more from Winnipeg when we got home. The two producers used almost a year's worth of footage to create an eighty-minute documentary called *Beyond the Beat*. The two producers were so involved with our family they became our friends.

Meanwhile, the nominations catapulted Rob's music career to a new level. He started doing shows all over Canada and it not only supported his passion to become a full-time artist, but his work also supported our family. While opportunities came knocking to leave Winnipeg for bigger cities, Rob found his niche and calling at First Nations communities all over North America. It's on reserves, he said, that he found the greatest joy in bringing his music and message of hope. "Young people on reserves are the best to perform for," he told me once. "They appreciate live music more and really get into it when we're there. I found my calling there."

I called him a 'hope dealer,' after that. He said kids and teens on reserves are the most loving and receptive audiences he's ever performed for. "I feel like they need it, that they appreciate when new people come and hang out with them. They come out of their shyness and really get into the music," he'd tell people. His music did go on to be nominated for at least fifty more music awards throughout the years following, including the Junos. He remains a nominee in the mainstream awards, but he's won many other ones in gospel music awards and started to produce albums for new and emerging artists as well. Throughout all of it, we felt like we were partners. He helped me fulfill my dream and I helped him. But it wasn't always easy, and it got harder as fame grew along with his artistry.

Chapter 16

MY DREAM CAME TRUE TOO

As a child, I remember sitting on the lap of a great man visiting my dad and being enthralled by their conversation. I was nine years old when Elijah Harper came to visit our house in the middle of the night. Elijah was making a campaign stop in Bunibonibee while he was running to be the Member of Legislative Assembly for northern Manitoba that coming year. He drove in on the winter road and arrived after we all went to bed.

That one night, I clearly remember the knock on the door and my dad answering it and being very happy to greet whoever it was. I stayed in bed at first, but curiosity got the best of me. I heard the low voices and occasional laugh, I wanted to be a part of it. I went down the hall slowly, not sure if my dad would tell me to go back to bed. But as soon as Elijah noticed me, he smiled a big smile and said hello. "This is Sheila," my dad told Elijah. Elijah reached out and said come here, and he put me on his lap as my dad finished pouring tea for the both of them. They sat for a while talking about family and politics.

My dad asked Elijah at one point, "What is Howard Pawley like?"

I don't remember Elijah's full answer, but he did say, "Pawley's a good man, he's okay."

"That's good," my dad replied.

This would have been around the time both my dad and Elijah were Chiefs, and both knew all the Indigenous and non-Indigenous leaders of that time. Since that visit, I loved being a part of storytelling. I mostly listened but I knew I could retell stories, especially ones of current affairs and politics.

It was from then on that I remember being more impressed with my parents for knowing all these people we would see and hear about on CBC News. CBC was the only channel we had for many years in Bunibonibee and the people telling the stories became my role models. Ones I wanted to emulate. Again, the supper-hour news anchor Sandra Lewis was one my favourites, but I also loved seeing Knowlton Nash. Later on, I admired people like Coleen Rajotte, Rick Ratte, and Jim Compton, some of the first Indigenous storytellers I noticed on the news. Their work fascinated me and I wanted to be like them.

I grew up wanting to be in the thick of conversations and be able to relay the stories to other people. I gobbled up all the news and current affairs shows I saw, like the *Fifth Estate*, *The National*, and local newscasts. Even though I didn't necessarily understand what the issues were, I appreciated learning about the news around the world. This of course was when I was still living in an isolated community where we as a family and community rarely left to go anywhere. The costs to leave for any reason were too high. The views on the TV was the closest I got to knowing what the world was doing outside Bunibonibee.

I dreamed one day I would be part of the storytelling world I saw. But it wasn't until I started helping Rob go after his dreams that I started to remember my own dreams of becoming a journalist. I would talk about it with him and he didn't seem to have any doubts that I could become a reporter. "I can't wait to see you on my TV and on billboards," Rob would say. I would laugh a little, not really convinced it could really happen. But I appreciated the encouragement. And it became a reality, the TV part, not the billboards, yet. My parents also used to make me feel like a big shot too, I felt invincible. "You will be good, you know what to do," they'd say. Or, "You are smart, you will get to where you are wanting to go." At a time when I wasn't sure of myself or my future, Rob helped me gain enough self-confidence to start thinking about a career in journalism. I even started to change how I dressed and what I thought of myself. He helped me come out of the shell that I let my ex-husband put me in. Rob became my best friend and my main cheerleader in life.

Chapter 17

LIFE HURDLES

As Rob and I started pursuing and achieving some of our dreams, things got more complicated, as life usually does when you're married. In the first few years of our marriage, my children's and my lives revolved solely around Rob's life and music. We always had some sort of studio in our house, always had a visitor staying with us recording with Rob, going to music festivals and shows. Most of the shows were in Winnipeg, but once in a while we'd all tag along and go with Rob and other artists to shows throughout Canada and the United States. We made little vacations out of it.

As my children got into high school we stayed home more as Rob would go off on tours with his fellow artists. He got so busy he needed managers to help him with bookings and scheduling. He started to make more money doing all the shows and appearances, but it got to a point where he was barely home five days a month. He got so exhausted one day he called saying he couldn't do it anymore. I felt so bad for him, I went to talk to the manager. I asked for Rob's schedule, saying neither of us knew where he was going next and when he'd be coming back. "Can I see the schedule you have for Rob? He's getting burnt out and wants to come home," I said to the manager. On one of the longest trips he had, he was gone about three months straight.

The manager kind of smirked at me dismissively and flat out told me to, "Get used to it!"

I told him Rob and I thought he was keeping Rob too busy.

He added, "Other artist's wives have to come to me to work out a time they can be with their husband's for special occasions, you can start there. In fact," he said, "marriages in the music business don't last long. I'm surprised you two are still together!"

We were married about seven years at this point. That was a huge wake up call. When I told Rob about that conversation, it was the end of that partnership, even though it had become a lucrative venture.

Despite the fallout with managers and friends who came and went during that time, Rob kept going. He started booking his own shows and went on the road to shows he wanted to do. He'd still be gone for weeks, but this time the trips were made on terms we could deal with. During those years, my children became teens and we ended up living life by ourselves again. We got into a routine, but there were moments life got really challenging, usually the hardships had to do with a shortage of money.

After our first trip to the Grammys, I was accepted into Red River College (RRC) and University of Winnipeg's Creative Communications program. I was nervous but I knew I needed to do the course to move from being a radio DJ to TV journalist. I wasn't sure if I should quit NCI to go back to school, so I deferred the acceptance for a year and took a few courses at U of W to keep my name in the program. When I finally decided to go to Red River College in 2004, I got right into it and loved being back in school full time.

To help with bills I kept my job at NCI and recorded Cree/English shows in the evenings a day ahead while I took classes during the day. Thankfully, my work at NCI allowed me to gain valuable experience in the broadcast industry so I was able to bypass a few courses and got credits for them instead. That allowed me to keep working at NCI part-time. I'm not quite sure how our little family kept up with everything we did then, but we managed. The kids were busy in sports and other programs, like acting and dancing. We were high functioning but tired all the time too! It was during my first few months in the creative communications program at RRC that we received word about Rob's second Grammy nomination. It was again, surreal.

In 2005, months before I graduated, I started working at CBC Winnipeg. I was there as an intern first, and weeks later I went back to start as a casual reporter. I also interned for a summer at CTV Winnipeg in between my first and second year of school. I met so many amazing reporters and people from the industry then, some of whom are still my good friends today. I also had an offer to work full time at APTN that summer. I had applied for an opening I saw for a part time job there. The producer who interviewed me wanted me to leave college and work there instead. I was fully prepared to work there, but on a part time basis.

"I'd like to finish school first before I go full time though," I said.

"Why," she asked, sounding annoyed. "You can learn on the job here; you can start tomorrow."

I turned her down again and she didn't like that. In fact, she was mad that I was passing up the opportunity. She told me that I'd never get an opportunity like that again. She was right, at least at APTN. Every time I applied at APTN for other opportunities, even up until now, I was never chosen. Sometimes people assume I've worked at APTN, but I never have. Though of course I wanted to.

I did get an opportunity at CBC though. My internship turned into a full-time job two years after being a casual reporter and I stayed at CBC until 2012. I was technically in college when I started the internship, months after the APTN producer scolded me for turning their job down. This time I felt more prepared to take a job in the industry, but it meant I had to make a choice between finishing classes or taking the offer at CBC. I took the casual job, and the college honoured my work and experience with enough credits to graduate. I was very happy. When I started Rob and I laughed about the time he told me years earlier that I would be working at CBC someday.

Chapter 18

ME AS A JOURNALIST

When I started at CBC, I was adamant that I only wanted to tell stories that affected the greater public. I didn't want to be known as that 'Native reporter.' I wanted to tell stories about potholes, street openings, cat fashion shows, anything that would appeal to all viewers. I thought that was the only good type of journalist, one who was able to tell mainstream stories. I realized later that much of my hesitation about telling any stories about diversity, adversity, or anything Indigenous was about me trying to avoid being subject to ridicule and racism for being Cree.

But it was impossible to avoid racism, especially long-engrained systemic racism. Even in journalism school and of course the newsrooms when I first started were teeming with it. Most of it was not overt racism or mean-spirited but it did not feel good to come up against it. Sometimes I didn't even recognize racism or systemic racism for what it was. For instance, I was used to introducing myself with a "Tansi, I'm Sheila North," when I worked as an announcer at NCI radio. When I started at CBC, I had a habit of introducing myself the same way with a 'Tansi' (which means hello in English) when I was doing live hits on the newscasts or in promos of stories. I noticed that 'Tansi' would be cut off. I didn't have enough confidence then to ask why, but a producer had more than enough of it to tell me not to use the Cree greeting anymore. The producer said it was too confusing and we didn't have enough time in the programs to explain what it meant. I complied even though I felt bad that I went against what my parents had taught me: to not call attention to myself, to not offend people or sound or seem like I was being disrespectful. Imposing my Cree language and perspectives felt like that sometimes. It felt like there was no time or room for me as a Cree person, only time and space for me as a person who didn't cause problems. I imagine that's the same type of messaging Indian Residential School survivors and thrivers got when they first started at residential schools in years past.

When I was still in college, we had to do an exercise where we were to watch all the local news programs for a week and make observations about them. Pointing out differences and similarities. One similarity I noticed was that if you closed your eyes and only listened to the stories, no matter what station, the voices were all very similar. Similar in tone, volume, and no detection of diversity. Everyone sounded white. Nothing wrong with sounding white, if you are. But what I was noticing was that there was little or no room for diverse voices, especially ones with an accent of any kind. There were diverse faces of course, but all of them and us in college were taught to speak a certain way, mainstream. I understand part of the thinking was to keep any tone of bias out of stories journalists told. But it didn't always feel right to do that as some stories and situations do need added perspectives from various cultural groups.

During the years I was a journalist and ever since, I've seen the look and sound of Canadian media personalities start to change. Instead of asking reporters to abandon what made them unique or leave out perspectives of what makes them who they are, storytellers are being asked to tap into their communities to provide context and contacts for more stories. Over time, I think newsrooms started to realize the way stories were being delivered needed to change with the times.

I strongly believe social movements like Idle No More and Black Lives Matter helped change the attitudes in the media outlets as well. Along with that, the rise in social media, giving some power to virtually anyone on it, helped change the media landscape. Almost overnight, people were telling their own stories in their own voices. This forced journalists and newsrooms to compete with average people in how stories were being told. But I think it also emboldened journalists to be more like their true selves and to not put up with racism anymore, much like the people they were telling stories about.

Instead of people being asked to tone down their cultural identities, journalists, hosts, and other on-air talents are now encouraged to have diversity to come through.

There are still, of course, problems—racism is less tolerated but still prevalent in many systems and in many minds because racism has been taught through the Canadian education system since the beginning of what is now Canada. Inevitably, some in the media, as in many other systems, still harbour racist views that come through in stories now and again. This is part of colonization that I feel we are finally starting to dismantle. Slowly but surely.

I also remember having a hard time meeting deadlines when I first started because I felt more comfortable listening to interviews more than once to get the full meaning of the answers. I felt better hearing answers once in English and then listening again at least twice more to interpret in my own head what was being said into my first language, Cree. Especially when it came to personal thoughts or the complex stories that I seemed to be telling more of. I wanted to get the true essence of what the person I was interviewing was saying. Obviously, listening more than once to interviews meant that I took longer to do my reporting than other seasoned journalists and my way was not always ideal for day-to-day reporting where you have to be quick and decisive. I got better I think, but it took me a while to get there. Meantime, I went home crying a few times because I felt like a failure and wanted to quit when I missed deadlines.

One of the times I did go home was after a manager pulled me aside and told me to get it together. I was finishing up a sad story about a tragic death when I got a call about another incident. I wanted someone to help me finish the technical aspects of filing a story for television and radio so I could start gathering information about the next story that landed in my lap. I think the impression I was giving off was that I didn't want to do the technical part of my job, that perhaps I thought I was too good to do that part of the job, or I was too lazy. But I felt the opposite of that, I was vibrating, full of eagerness to keep gathering stories that people were opening up to me about. I didn't want sources to feel I didn't have time for them or didn't care about what they wanted to tell me.

Either way, I think my supervisor may have been tasked to try to encourage me to work faster and do all aspects of the job no matter what else was on the go. I believe the supervisor was simply trying to give me what I'll call 'tough love.' He said, "You're never going to be a great reporter because you're not vain enough, you're not fast enough or you're not mean enough. So just do your job." I thought I was. The supervisor said more than that, but the rest of it faded as I retreated. I didn't know how to take that at first, but it made me feel completely inadequate. I grabbed my personal things and left his office in a huff without saying goodbye to anyone. But as soon as I was outside, I cried and went home.

When I got home I stayed there for a few days. I talked to my husband about it and he was very sympathetic and patient with me. He said everything would be okay, but I was pretty sure I was done. I didn't want to go back to the newsroom. What I was told to be like was not who I was. My personality was more about being quiet, not bringing attention to myself and definitely not being competitive. If it were not for a couple of my colleagues at the time who called me, I might never have gone back to try again. I was at home for about three days and I didn't even explain to anyone at work what I was feeling. I didn't know how. Then I got a call from two of my colleagues who seemed to understand how I felt and told me it was hard, but I was capable of doing the job. I didn't really believe it, but they encouraged me to get my butt back into the newsroom and just do my best. I did that and I don't regret that decision. I still value the conversations I had during that time, even the one with the supervisor!

Two of the people who encouraged me are Crystal Goomansingh, now a journalist based in London, England and Cynthia Kent who now lives in Ontario. They inspired me, most people I worked with at CBC and CTV inspired me and encouraged me. In fact, they inspired me so much that I got pretty good at getting stories that other reporters couldn't get. I became known as one of the most enterprising journalists in Manitoba. But that was toward the end of my career in reporting.

My parents were also very encouraging of my career as a journalist, though sometimes they did have some comments on my reporting style! I was assigned to do a cold weather story. The temperature dipped into the minus 40's and I was on a road showing how hard the snow was blowing. I did a live standup, meaning I was on the air on the CBC supper-hour newscast talking to the host about how cold it was. There

I was, hair blowing in the wind and trying not to wince from the cold. When I was done, my cellphone rang. It was my dad calling and I could hear my mom talking in the background too as I said, "hello."

"Sheila," Dad said in his usual stern and loud low voice, like he'd sound when I was in trouble as a kid!

"Hi Dad," I said, curious to hear what he had to say.

"I just saw you on TV," he bellowed.

At first, I thought he was going to say he loved seeing me on TV, like he'd done many times before that.

This time though he followed up with, "You weren't wearing a hat! It's cold out there, why aren't you wearing a hat?" he asked as my mom in the background was telling him to tell me I should be wearing a hat.

"I am now, Dad," I said. "I just took it off for a minute to be on TV."

"Well, keep in on," he said.

"Okay, Dad," I replied.

I had a good chuckle after that, but I always made sure I looked prepared in any standup from then on, so Mom and Dad wouldn't worry when they saw me in any harsh conditions. They were so sweet though, my mom told me that she and Dad would sometimes sit and cry with happy tears when they saw me reporting on TV. Mom said it felt like they were on TV with me, and they were. I carried them in my heart and mind in everything I've done and still do. And I realized a long time ago that I was never too old for a good scolding from them once a while, which I still love to this day.

But not everyone had accepted my on-air presence so easily. On one of those early reporting days, I was on assignment covering a story about membership issues at a public pool. The staff accommodated us to talk to patrons and we saw one person in the pool, so my cameraman and I went to talk to him. While my camera guy was setting up the man in the pool started chit-chatting and said, "I guess you can't come in the pool because of your mukluks." Of course, it was in the middle of summer, I wasn't wearing mukluks! Duh! But his stupidity made me laugh! When I got back to the newsroom, the same manager who'd attempted to give me tough love, called the gym and berated them for allowing that kind of talk in a public space like that. The gym said they couldn't control that.

After a few months of being an intern journalist, I felt that I had no choice but to speak up because I felt there weren't enough stories that reflected the authentic Indigenous perspectives. It wasn't evident to me anyway. As I started to pay more attention to the newscasts as a whole and being in story pitching meetings, I felt the need, the calling, to listen closer and say what Indigenous people around me were truly saying. I worked as a Cree radio announcer for Manitoba's largest Indigenous radio station that covered the entire province before I started at CBC. While there, I had a chance to learn and understand what Indigenous people were saying, what they were mostly interested in, and what they liked and didn't like. I appreciated my time at NCI, most of the time it was a lot of fun to work there. But I didn't realize I was gaining so much knowledge about our people in that time as well.

From my experience at NCI and staying connected to the community, as well as growing up in Bunibonibee, I was able to bring some Indigenous perspectives as I knew them to CBC. And I was able to compare that with what I was seeing and hearing in my new role at CBC and other media outlets as well. I felt that we as media had to show how Indigenous people really are. Not just subjects of sad or tragic stories. We are people who feel the impact of the stories told about us. At the time—even today—many stories reinforced negative stereotypes about Indigenous people. Some incited hate towards them, not just Indigenous people but all marginalized groups. I started to look around and ask myself how I was contributing to that. Thinking about that gave me a greater sense of responsibility to speak up and share the perspectives I knew and understood.

At that time, racism was even tolerated on news websites. I cringed every time I'd read responses to stories about Indigenous people. Many of the comments told us as Indigenous people to, "Go back to where you came from." That was my favourite (insert sarcasm here!). Other comments included keyboard cowboys posting about how lazy, irresponsible, and dumb Indigenous people were, for example. It was very disheartening to read that about our people at the place where I worked. I didn't find peace on that issue until I made a decision not to read the comment sections of any media outlet site because doing so was discouraging and hurtful. I still don't read those comments, I feel better that way. That was how it was then; however, I think most news websites now monitor the comment sections for hate speech and the like. The change seemed slow, but the change became more noticeable when more Indigenous journalists came on the scene all over Canada and we started speaking louder about our concerns.

I started to see real changes in the newsroom as well. For example, all the reporters in the newsroom had to show up every day with new story ideas or new information about stories we'd already told that included diversity. All of us had to come up with at least one story idea that covered Indigenous issues or issues facing other people of colour. And, even if a story wasn't about people of colour, our stories had to include at least one person of colour speaking. I liked the new policy because we were all forced to think outside our own communities or ones we were used to. It was easy for me; the hard part was trying to convince fellow Indigenous people to talk to me on camera at first. Many Indigenous people and other people of colour didn't always trust the media or any place of 'authority.' So, I had to make an extra effort there too to get Indigenous people on camera. Now you can't stop us from speaking up, even on live news programs.

As you can imagine, most of the people working in the industry then and now have strong personalities and are confident and bold. We were taught and encouraged to 'speak truth to power,' to question everything. We were also taught to be respectful and mindful of all perspectives, especially those opposite of our own. I appreciate the lessons I learned during my time as a reporter. Learning the skills of being a reporter also helped me years later when I was pulled into politics as a candidate. I learned how to process information quicker, to be more decisive, and how to present information in a calm, professional manner.

My time with CBC toughened me up in many ways, taught me to speak up and not be afraid of anyone or anything. This was different from what my parents taught me, which was not to complain, not to question authority, to make the best of what I was given, not to ask for more of anything, and not to brag. Of course, my parents taught me other strong loving attributes. Besides all the leadership lessons I learned from

Dad, Mom taught me to value myself as a person, to be tremendously self-disciplined, to be grateful and mindful of others and of what I had in life. What they and many Indigenous people were taught through colonization, was to feel inferior to white people or people with power. In being a reporter and eventually an elected leader, I had to find a balance of all the invaluable lessons I learned from my parents, my ex, and my colleagues at CBC. But sometimes these values clashed and shook my confidence or deflated it altogether. However, I like to see myself as a thriver now, and I value every lesson I've learned in my time as a journalist and from everyone I've met and worked with. Journalism was my dream, and the work exceeded all my expectations of the job. Still does. I love being a storyteller.

Chapter 19

BECOMING SEASONED

During my about ten combined years of reporting at CBC, CTV, and NCI I strived to have a neutral voice. I never aligned myself with any mainstream political party or special interest group—though I was almost convinced once to run as a candidate in the pandemic election of 2021. I was taught in journalism school to be impartial, and I feel for the most part I was. But being neutral didn't mean deaf or shutting off my feelings. Several times I felt like I had to speak out when fellow journalists or news decision-makers seemed to be shortsighted or misrepresenting Indigenous people. But speaking out as a reporter, especially as a reporter who happened to be an Indigenous woman, sometimes got me in trouble when I questioned people in positions of power.

One of these times was with a Winnipeg Police Service spokesperson. Three times in a row he berated me in front of other reporters. I had talked to WPS spokespeople many times before and none of them had ever talked the way he did to me. He didn't like me questioning him or the police in any way, it wasn't the first time I interacted with him either. It was my job to ask questions, but he made it seem like I was asking questions for petty reasons.

One of the last times the spokesperson berated me was about a fight at a hockey rink and whether the referee who broke an Indigenous boy's arm was a son of a police officer, which is what the boy's team officials believed. The officials at the time were concerned the referee wouldn't be fully investigated if there was a connection to the police force. I asked the spokesperson about whether or not a member's son was the referee. Instead of giving me a cordial answer, the spokesperson accused me of always looking to try and to find racists! "You're always looking for trouble like that eh, Sheila?" he said. "Always accusing us of being racist."

But I wasn't: stories about racism and racist behaviours were finding me. I had my cameraman in the vehicle with me when the spokesperson was yelling at me, and he heard it all as well. From that time on until I was done working as a journalist, that same spokesperson treated me with disrespect. It was clear he didn't like me.

It's not surprising that the relationship between police and Indigenous people in Winnipeg and throughout Canada has been difficult. There have been trust issues and that tense relationship still needs a lot of work. All I know is the police didn't like to be questioned, which is part of the nature of their jobs perhaps. But my job when I was a reporter was to ask questions, no matter how difficult or awkward they were. My time in newsrooms and particularly with seasoned station managers helped me gain the confidence to do that.

Another awkward situation with WPS happened when I was telling stories about a group of reforming street gang members who were trying to transition from a life of crime to living without crime. There was a transition house that some wanted to go to after leaving jail and before moving home with family or friends. But the guys running the transition house felt the WPS was not giving them a fair shake and was constantly raiding the house. At the end of the day, it was a 'he said, he said' story. I'm sure there was some truth to both sides, but I was telling the side that not all reporters were comfortable telling and apparently members of the WPS were not happy with me. A well-respected man within the police force phoned me out of the blue and said, "Listen, Sheila. Police don't like you. Whatever you do, do it right. I wouldn't even jaywalk if I was you," he said. It was unnerving because it felt like the police were trying to discredit me in any way they could.

Coincidentally, my brake lines were cut during that time as well. A mechanic said they were clearly cut. I'll never know who did that, but my suspicion is someone who knew what they were doing. When I talked to one of my bosses at CBC about it, he said, "Consider it a compliment that the police are paying attention to your work. It means you may be getting closer to the truth." I left his office, feeling a little jarred at first, but as his words sunk in, they empowered me. I felt like I was starting to understand the world even better and saw a glimpse of what it was like to be so sure of myself. I started to feel less scared or leery of police and people in authority. Instead, I felt like I was doing my job. Holding people accountable as a journalist.

More confidence helped me help my husband Rob speak out about a time he was being racially profiled while driving his white Chrysler 300. He was stopped at gunpoint in the middle of traffic and was asked to prove he was driving his own car. It was a fiasco! He was seen driving it and I guess the police officer saw him and became suspicious that he had stolen the car. It was unbelievable.

"Hey babe, you'll never believe what just happened to me," Rob said in a rushed tone.

"What," I said, sensing his intensity.

"I just got pulled over. Cops had their guns out, got me out of the car and had me lie on the ground. They accused me of stealing my car," he added.

After he told me that, I told a radio producer I was working with at CBC.

"Tell him to come by if he wants to tell his story," he said.

I told Rob to come to CBC to see me. That very afternoon another reporter told his story. The incident eventually made headlines everywhere. What helped in making the news headlines was that he was a Grammy-nominated artist who became well known in the community. Without his local celebrity status, I think at the time police would've found a way to say their actions were justified. The police officers who had him on the ground were young, Rob said. And the impression he got from them was that they were trying to prove themselves. "One of them held a gun sideways, like in gangster movies," he said. At that time, the Winnipeg mayor had Rob as a co-chair of his re-election campaign. In the end, Winnipeg police officials apologized to Rob.

Sadly, when they were young, my children saw with their own eyes WPS members attacking their father in the middle of the street. The story they tell me is that they were crossing the street and a police car pulled up and immediately began questioning my ex-husband. Instead of waiting for answers from him, the police officers took turns kicking and punching him in front of my children, who were terrified. No wonder our children and Indigenous people everywhere have a deep mistrust for police officers and police agencies.

The worst encounter I had with people wearing badges was at the Canadian/American border. One of my sisters and I were going for a daytrip to the States, and we were pulled for further screening by the border agents. They ripped our car apart and found nothing. My sister and I didn't know the process and when I asked if we had to put everything back together, one officer got really mad about the question. Once we were done putting everything back together, we drove off, squealed off actually. We were driving a little rental and we just wanted to get out of there. Turns out the little car had some zip.

The one officer who really made it clear he didn't like us, yelled for us to stop. We stopped and he and others ran towards us surrounding our car, yelling at us to get out. We rolled the windows down and tried to talk to them, but as soon as I opened my window the same mad officer pulled me out of the car by grabbing me by my head. I couldn't see what was happening to my sister behind us, but she started to cry. Meanwhile, the officer who pulled me out of the car was whispering in my ear as he hiked up my wrists up toward my shoulder blades walking toward the border agency building. He was whispering things like, "You're garbage, you're a piece of shit, you're a bitch." I didn't say anything back. I was actually taken back in my mind to all the stories I heard as a journalist and from others, including family who told me of their experiences with police brutality. It seemed like a long walk to the building. As we entered the building, he started pulling me back and forth saying loudly, "Quit resisting, quit resisting!" It was like something straight out of a movie. All I could think to say was, "I'm not." Though I think I called him a punk too.

It took about an hour for the other agents to sort things out while my sister and I were held in separate rooms and searched again and asked a lot of questions. At one point I told the officers that we were Cree people with Treaty Status and that the Jay Treaty between Canada and the US allowed us to travel back and forth without problems. I didn't know if that was completely accurate at that time but one of them listened. I could hear that same officer tell the mad agent that we were Status Indians. He said, "I don't care." At that moment he was told to go home. He didn't sound happy about that and stormed off in a huff. Minutes later we were told we weren't being charged with anything and allowed to go. They didn't explain why were suddenly let go, but the incident definitely had something to do with our race because we saw a Muslim family being treated similarly in the rooms next to us.

Outside of the building, my sister cried some more. I was too stunned to cry! We sat in the car for a bit before leaving, comparing the marks on our wrists. We wanted to file a complaint, but in the end everyone we talked to told us not to make trouble otherwise we'd be put on an American no-entry list. We let it go.

There are other examples of police overstepping their authority and beating people up that I know of. Incidents that have happened to some of my own family members. It's not my place to tell their stories, but I will say the incidents were brutal and could have led to death.

Chapter 20

FROM THE CBC TO ADVOCACY

In my earlier days as a journalist, I avoided stories about my own people and issues affecting us. I realized later I was ignoring my true calling, to share the perspectives of Indigenous people. Instead, I learned to tolerate racism and not to speak up against it. We, as a country, including myself, were taught to ignore, disrespect, and disregard the First People of this country. No one expressly told me not to tell stories affecting Indigenous people or any other ones about diversity, I just felt I shouldn't if I wanted to be successful. But it didn't take long to realize that I had to share the Indigenous perspectives that I knew.

Towards the end of the seven years of the first time I worked for CBC, I was less tolerant of racism—both overt and systemic. More people were speaking out and social justice movements were emerging, including those demanding an end to not knowing what was happening to so many missing and murdered Indigenous women, girls, and people. There were calls for justice to protect the lands and resources, calls for protection and assertion of Treaty and Aboriginal Rights, and calls for greater respect and dignity for Indigenous people in general. As the calls for justice were becoming louder, some of the stories about the reasons for the calls were hard to hear. Stories of racism, of life and death situations, and of enough hardships for many lifetimes were particularly difficult. This was just as the Truth and Reconciliation Commission was beginning its work in 2008, gathering and documenting stories about Residential School experiences in Canada. All of the stories and voices were amplified in living rooms across the country through the media on all platforms including all the traditional supper-hour news programs.

The TRC was established as part of the Indian Residential Schools Settlement Agreement and after Canadian Prime Minister Stephen Harper issued an apology on behalf of Canada to all Indian Residential School survivors. I've had to translate the apology into Cree for a show on the schools called *We Were Children* by Lisa Meeches and others from the Eagle Vision production company. It was pretty grueling to do. I wasn't expecting it to be as hard to do as it was, and it was particularly hard when I translated the part of the speech when Mr. Harper said, "To kill the Indian in the child."

This was the speech that the Conservative Prime Minister had to deliver at that time because of the calls by many advocates demanding an apology from the Canadian government for its role in establishing residential schools across the country. The speech came before the TRC could do its work, as part of a truth telling exercise that many former students, survivors, families, leaders, and advocates were calling for. It was a significant step and all of the leaders from national Indigenous advocacy organizations were present, including AFN National Chief Phil Fontaine, one of the former students who was instrumental in negotiating an apology and reaching a settlement agreement between the federal government and former residential school students/survivors/thrivers. The apology touched on very important and necessary points that needed to be said. But for me and many others, the seven words that stuck out was the description of the main purpose of residential schools: "To Kill the Indian in the Child."

It took great effort for me to try and think of Cree words or terms to explain that concept. When you translate into Cree, it's more about the essence of words or sentences, the main aspects of the ideas in sentences are more important than the exact words. In trying to explain what 'to kill the Indian in the child' meant, I had to think of my late grandparents. I was wondering how I would try to explain that line to them and broke down. I was thinking of the gravity of the phrase, the intent to get rid of the beautiful and powerful Original People of these lands, people like my relatives and everyone I knew growing up in Bunibonibee. I sat in the dark little sound booth sobbing for a few minutes. I had to regain my composure before continuing.

Slowly, I noticed attitudes and language by the public and media start-ing to change. Indigenous people were speaking up louder and pushing back against media and other systems that negatively impacted their lives, including political ones. Many did so through social media platforms. With social media, people's voices were being heard in their own words, and it became impossible for conventional media and the greater public to ignore those words. Movements of change were renewed, most notably calls for an inquiry into Missing and Murdered Indigenous Women (MMIW) and Girls (MMIWG) and Idle No More that began as a way to push back against the Harper Conservative government's Omnibus Budget Bill C-45, which being proposed at that time. The bill could've had significant negative impact Indigenous Peoples' rights.

The increasing awareness of MMIW and overt and covert racist attitudes, inspired many to get involved in the movements, including me. This is when I went from being a journalist to being an advocate! It wasn't part of my plan; it was the wave of change that caught me in its currents and hasn't let me go since.

I was also becoming less tolerant of bullies. Before leaving my dream job at CBC, a fellow Indigenous journalist took opportunities when no one else was listening to make fun of me and my upbringing in a Christian home. He would walk by and sarcastically say, "Oh hallelujah." Or he'd ask, "Is your husband still doing that hallelujah rap?" This former colleague was trying to be a rapper at the time too. My husband told me not to say anything back and I think he dropped off a Christian rap CD for the reporter once at work.

It wasn't the first time I was made fun of because of my upbringing in church. It happened when I was child too at home in Bunibonibee and in Brandon at college. I was used to it, and I even understand why some people would have those views about church and Indigenous people who go to church, but it certainly didn't feel good to be on the receiving end of their disdain for churches or religion. I couldn't help growing up that way, and I value my upbringing.

I do understand why some Indigenous people think negatively about 'church' and 'Christianity.' Some will even say they hate church and Christianity. I get that too. There was a lot of harm done to Indigenous people through colonization, and it was organized religion that settlers used to justify their genocidal actions toward Indigenous people and their lands and resources. Many people were harmed, and some died at the hands of church leaders. It was most obvious during the Residential School era when Indigenous children were taken from their families and placed in church-run, government-mandated institutions. During the day, students were taught about the 'love of God' and at night, the clergy and other school staff sexually assaulted children.

The concept of 'the Doctrine of Discovery' is another obvious example of how the church, predominantly the Roman Catholic Church and its Papal system, was used to justify European settlers' claim to lands and resources originally inhabited by Indigenous people on Turtle Island. The doctrine of discovery was ultimately used to form Canada as the country, the state that it is now. A country that ultimately dismissed, and still dismisses, the right and titles of Indigenous people to their lands and resources. So certainly, religion and church has had deep and lasting impacts on Indigenous people. The presence of the church has changed the course of history for Indigenous people, and I believe we are still working at regaining what we have lost in the colonial systems imposed on our people. It's not a wonder that some don't like the church and people who go to church!

For me, church was a constant in my life. My parents met in church, both of them had experiences like many Indigenous people that could have caused them to lose hope and struggle in life in many ways. Instead, they chose to incorporate church and the Bible into their lives and as parents. Through church and the Bible, they taught me and my siblings about discipline, love, patience, and forgiveness, for example. Going to church to me was about having a personal relationship with God our Creator, who I believe in human form was Jesus.

The church we went to was also Apostolic, not Catholic. In fact, I've only been to about two Catholic church services. A big difference in my view because the church life I was a part of was more about family and community support. Most of the services were spoken in Cree and so were the songs. Sure, there were teachings about how there is only one way to get to heaven and only one way to worship God, but as an adult looking at the bigger picture my views about that have changed. I still value the way I was taught about Creator and will cherish my time with family growing up in church, but I think people who believe in other ways are also right and deserve respect.

While people wonder why some Indigenous people would engage in organized religion, I don't think the differences in opinion is reason enough to bully or ridicule someone else for how they believe and how they choose to worship. Dealing with a co-worker about this wasn't new though. In Brandon, I met some fellow students who grew up learning only about the Traditional Ways. They too were very strong in their faith, but they weren't always kind in telling me I was wrong for going to church or believing in God the way I did.

Spirituality is a personal thing in one's life, and I think there are already enough hardships in life that we don't need to debate about who's right. I think we all just need to do our best to live life in a good way. God, Creator, Jesus—however you choose to acknowledge the Great Spirit—will figure it out.

What made things worse about the Indigenous colleague who was bullying me about Christianity was that he was also getting amazing opportunities at work. Opportunities of advancement that I or other Indigenous colleagues would have appreciated and had earned as well. No doubt he had talent and abilities, but there were some of us who had been there longer. To me it was a slap in the face. Especially since I gave my heart and soul to my job, to the corporation. I worked hard even after work hours, driven by the need to get the stories on the air. But after seeing the quick advancement of one colleague over others, I started to lose my passion to 'get the good gets.'

I was proud of all the stories I was telling, and I was proud of our people speaking out more, but I was getting burnt out. Then in 2012, my friend Jennifer Wood and another advisor to the new Assembly of Manitoba Chiefs (AMC) Grand Chief, then Derek Nepinak, made me an offer I couldn't turn down. They wanted me to be the chief communications officer for the Grand Chief. I wasn't sure I knew what the job entailed but I accepted the offer, also in part because of my frustrations at CBC.

Chapter 21

WORKING FOR MURDERED AND MISSING INDIGENOUS WOMEN AND GIRLS

The work I did with the new AMC Grand Chief was new to me. I didn't know what exactly he and the organization wanted me to do. I asked to meet with him to see if he could tell me and he simply said, "Just do what you do." I had to figure out what that was myself by monitoring current events and suggesting to the Grand Chief what to respond to in the media and what not to. He was hesitant to speak to the media at first, but when I told him what to expect in interviews and what questions would possibly come up, he quickly gained confidence and became one of the most quoted and visible Indigenous leaders in Canada.

The training and work I did as a journalist taught me to be assertive and decisive and gave me the ability to look at the bigger picture of any situation. I didn't realize I had those skills until I had to tap into them for the work I did with AMC. I also knew how to present ideas in a way that journalists and media would respond to. Along with my journalistic prowess, I realized that my maternal instincts and having survived an abusive relationship gave me the ability to speak up for others. From all of that, I feel I was able to understand what Indigenous people were saying when they started to mobilize across the country for greater justice.

I did see some disconnects during that time from all kinds of places. Some vocal First Nations Chiefs were passionate, but they also seemed clueless when they were dealing with families, survivors, and advocates of women and girls. When frustrations were getting high, some of these family members, survivors, and advocates would say they didn't want Chiefs to be involved in their calls for change because they felt like some men, including Indigenous men, were and are part of the problem. I saw both sides and each had valid concerns. Some female Chiefs told me that it was hard to bring up issues impacting women and girls because male Chiefs would tell them to take those discussions away from the main Chief's tables—that it was just women's issues.

Seeing, hearing, and feeling all of that I had to find a way to help the Chiefs and the families/survivors/advocates of MMIW find common ground. I felt the fight for justice had to include the greater public, but it would be hard to engage average citizens if we couldn't find a way to work together. I saw the bigger picture and the importance of bringing all those voices and perspectives together in order to inspire real changes in our society, such as changes for greater justice, respect, and dignity for Indigenous people.

It was all about human bridge-building at that time and to do that I had to absorb certain ideals and words that would set back relationships if I hadn't. For example, I was trying to engage one particularly strong MMIW family member and advocate, Bernadette Smith, to come and talk to Chiefs about the issue. She was always strong and vocal about the topic when I was working at CBC. In fact, she was one of the ones who pushed back at the media and told them, "If you don't name my sister and quit calling her a street worker, I won't talk to you." Her stance and that of similar advocates forced the media to change their tones forever.

In my initial meeting with my new boss Grand Chief Nepinak, I told him that I was a survivor of MMIW and that the issue is always with me, that I probably would always work at raising awareness about it. He told me that was good and encouraged me to keep being an advocate. In doing so, I thought it was important to ask Bernadette to come in and talk to Chiefs about the issue too. Her initial response was no. She said "they've [chiefs] never helped us before so I don't need to talk to them." The discussion was very much in the public eye at this time, more girls and women, including pregnant ones, were showing up dead on streets across Canada. Media was telling stories about it almost every day. I felt we all needed to get together as grassroots people and First Nations leaders and be on the same page, to have a stronger voice together.

When Bernadette refused to come in and speak to the Chiefs, I asked her for a compromise. I asked if she'd be willing to talk by phone at least, to join us on a conference call. She agreed. On the Chiefs' side, Grand Chief Nepinak was ready to learn and talk and invited a few Chiefs to join the conversations. GC Nepinak was being asked more and more to speak about the issue and he wanted other Chiefs to weigh in as well. So, I arranged a call. I was happy to bring them all together and I wanted to facilitate the discussion, but I cringed several times when one Chief who joined us in the boardroom for the call spoke. It was Arlen Dumas, who was chief of Pukatawagan Cree Nation at the time.

After the short introductions, I invited Bernadette to share her concerns about MMIW and what she thought we could all do to help get greater awareness out. She was not afraid to speak her mind and questioned why the Chiefs were only on board to help now that the media was paying attention. "They weren't around when we really needed them," she told me. "Why would I try to help them now?" Eventually though, the meeting did happen, and some tough conversations were had.

Chief Dumas pushed back and asked, "Who do you think you are?" I punched the mute button because I didn't want Bernadette to hear him. I asked for calm and resumed the call. The discussion was hard, and I felt like I made a mistake in initiating the call in the first place. It seemed Chief Dumas was more worried about his ego, and he was taking exception to the fact a woman was telling him some truths. And he seemed to be the only one at the time to take such offense. In the end, the call was productive. I think it at least led to the first steps of grassroots people and leaders working together to call for justice, including calling for a national inquiry into missing and murdered Indigenous women and girls. After the call, Chief Dumas came up to me and made a joke about me being scared. But what he was seeing—and I didn't say it to him, I just let his comment slide—was that I was feeling a great sense of responsibility to set this relationship in place. It was awkward because I didn't want anyone to get offended or hurt. His attitude, and even Bernadette's, didn't make it easy, but the conversation needed to happen if we were going to get anywhere.

From that time, Grand Chief Nepinak continued to learn more and more about the issue and was more comfortable talking about it in the media, especially when women and girls kept going missing or were found dead and there was a thought that there was a serial killer on the loose. It did feel like that; just weeks before, Shawn Lamb was arrested and charged with killing three young women: Lorna Blacksmith, Tanya Nepinak, and Carolyn Sinclair. Turned out that Derek Nepinak was related to one of the victims, Tanya Nepinak, so the issue was brought closer to home for him.

After the arrest of Shawn Lamb, more rallies about MMIW started happening. I helped from the Chiefs' side to suggest speakers and possible places for the rallies. Slowly, grassroots people started inviting Chiefs to speak at the gatherings and calls for justice grew louder to the point that in 2015 the issue of MMIW became a national election issue.

Being able to see people come together on such difficult discussions motivated me to keep working, to keep trying to bring people together for the greater good. I see now that the work I was doing during that time and the new skills I was acquiring helped me eventually in my work as an elected leader myself. My husband Rob would tell me during that time that I was going to be a Grand Chief myself, but of course I didn't really believe it. I couldn't see what he saw. To me I was just doing my job.

My job at the time was made easier because I was working with Grand Chief Nepinak, who had trained as a lawyer. He already knew the issues, so it was just a matter of helping him understand the media. Before long, he became the go-to person for any Indigenous issue that came up after 2012 until he finished his term in 2016. During this time, as more calls for an MMIW inquiry were ramping up, the Idle No More movement began. The tension between Indigenous people and the federal government under Prime Minister Stephen Harper was growing. There was less tolerance for what some Indigenous people saw as shortsighted racist policies and legislation that were coming out of government during the Harper administration. The biggest issues that caused tensions to rise and inspired Idle No More (INM) was around Harper's proposed Bill C-45. The bill affected over sixty federal government acts that were seen as eroding or diminishing Treaty and Aboriginal

Rights. The founders of INM, four women from Saskatchewan, Jessica Gordon, Sylvia McAdam, Sheelah McLean and Nina Wilson, were sounding the alarm on social media about what the passing of Bill C-45 could mean. The concern, in short, was that the Harper government was setting up new laws that would take the rights and title holders of lands and resources—Indigenous people—out of the conversations and decision-making processes. The bill would essentially make it easier for the government to build more pipelines, for example, without having to consult with First Nations who have special rights to lands and resources in Canada. The sovereignty of First Nations was under attack and the word about it all spread like wildfire on social media.

INM had a bit of a slow start at first but where I saw the movement picking up was when Chiefs started to get involved. Not to say it was the Chiefs who galvanized INM, but their support made governments pay attention to what the grassroots people were saying at the time.

It took a little longer for the Chiefs to get engaged in the movement. I, like many other technical support staff of the Chiefs from other Indigenous political organizations, was getting requests from INM organizers to get Chiefs involved. I honestly didn't know what to do with the information at first, but little by little as the founders of the movement kept talking, I started to catch on and began sharing the information with others. That year at the AFN annual winter assembly in Gatineau, Quebec, I talked with another communications person for a Saskatchewan Chief, and we decided to help bring the Chiefs and INM organizers together. We began with having press conferences together, calling for an end to Bill C-45.

I was still getting used to speaking out on my own thoughts because until then I'd only shared other people's views and reported on them. And for the most part I maintained that at least publicly, but behind the scenes I was helping by creating strategies to raise awareness about the MMIW and Idle No More movements and helping to empower people to speak out in the media on the topics. During this time at AMC, I created the hashtag #MMIW. I consulted with a woman who did a project on the issue and came up with the hashtag based on the need to highlight the problem while incorporating who was most impacted by the issue, Indigenous women. To me the word 'women' represented the whole female existence and experiences. And 'Indigenous' was more of an inclusive term for all Original People of these lands. That was the reasoning behind the hashtag after I thought about it for a while.

During the uprisings, I thought we all needed a common theme, the hashtag, to keep the conversations going on social media about ending violence against Indigenous women and girls. The hashtag naturally has extended versions of it as more people started using it. And when the Liberal government got into power in 2015 and made good on its promise to call an inquiry into missing and murdered women and girls, it used the hashtag #MMIWG. The extended hashtags and ones including men and boys are now widely used all over the world.

But it and the great awareness and movements of MMIW started on the streets and roads all over Canada, including Winnipeg. I am a witness to what is great about MMIW and how we all know what MMIW stands for. This because of all the champions, mostly women, girls, and their children who are family of MMIW or who were survivors of the epidemic and their advocates and allies, galvanized around the issue. There were also some men and boys who got involved and became relentless in making the issue known, but for the most part it was females who brought us all to this place of awareness now. This included people like Gail Nepinak (sister of Tanya Nepinak) and Cheryl James (a young single mom) who attended as many events as I could remember, drumming and singing at rallies, walks, and vigils. There were women like Bernadette Smith (sister of Claudette Osborne), Nahanni Fontaine, Diane Redsky and countless others who were working on justice issues in their own ways that helped mobilize the movement. Nationally, there were many others, of course, including Gladys Radek who walked several times across the country with her supporters calling for an end to MMIW. All the while, government officials and the police were dismissing the issue as a problem we as Indigenous people were causing ourselves.

The champions never gave up. They kept having public marches, rallies, and vigils for a good solid ten years across the country. Every time another woman or girl was declared missing or found murdered without a trace of the killer, the MMIW army mobilized. Sometimes there were only three people at an event, other times there were more than three thousand people marching together. The gatherings happened in all kinds of weather. Sometimes it was a really hot day, other days rainy or as cold as -30 degrees Celsius: it didn't seem to matter—the MMIW army didn't stop. Indigenous Peoples wouldn't allow MMIW, Idle No More, conditions on reserves, or other issues that negatively affected Indigenous Peoples to be ignored anymore. The voices got louder and stronger and media coverage grew to a point that issues Indigenous Peoples wanted the government to address were some of the top national election issues during the 2015 Canadian federal election. This was especially true of the MMIW movement, and leading up to the election each party had to answer whether or not they'd call an inquiry into the issue; the Conservatives didn't commit. Some in the party even blamed the victims and people for allowing the issue to exist and persist. Many Canadians agreed with them, but not all. Both the Liberals and the NDP at the time included MMIW in their platforms, committing to call an inquiry if they were elected. The loud voices on the streets that reached right into our living rooms every night and on our phones through social media made it virtually impossible to ignore Indigenous people.

When rallies and protests became more numerous across Canada, the media didn't quite know how to cover them at first. Eventually they were forced to do stories about the random public round dances that popped up in malls and streets. They were forced to cover the teach-ins and sit-ins at government offices and rallies in the cold outside of provincial legislative buildings. I remember one of the coldest days, December 10th, 2012, when a bunch of us were outside the Manitoba Legislature in Winnipeg holding an Idle No More rally. That night, watching the local news coverage, I was incensed to see the lead story was about the 'IKEA monkey.'

Granted it was cute to see a stranded monkey standing in a vestibule of an Ikea store wearing a double-breasted faux fur jacket! Even writing that sounds ridiculously funny. Though I wasn't laughing when I posted on Twitter that night that I was embarrassed that I ever worked in the media, since they didn't lead with the INM rally that night. One producer messaged me and tried to get me to admit the coverage was still good, but I disagreed. I told him that "people's lives are more important than that one monkey."

Not sure if everyone agrees, but nonetheless I did notice after that day the coverage of INM was taken more seriously by the media. Of course, seeing thousands of people gathering more and more that winter helped trigger more media coverage as well. I still remember the feeling of unity, power, and hope at some of the rallies, especially at one of the largest ones in Ottawa in front of Parliament Hill and the Prime Minister's Office on December 21st, 2012.

Even average Indigenous people were being impacted by the movements and feelings of unity and empowerment. I heard from people including family members not directly involved in the political scene say they felt a greater sense of respect when they were out in public. In Winnipeg, it wasn't and still is not unusual to feel discriminated against at any given time. It's no wonder *Maclean's* declared Winnipeg 'the most racist city in Canada' in 2015. But during the INM movement and greater calls to end violence against Indigenous people, the feeling of hope was everywhere. Many even used the INM movement as their own personal movement and highlighted issues that were important to them, not just the ones around Bill C-45.

That massive December rally in 2012 began after Stephen Harper refused to meet with Chiefs in their own circles at an Assembly of First Nations annual general meeting in Ottawa. The calls to meet Chiefs on their terms were heightened by the fact Theresa Spence, who was the Chief of Attawapiskat, Ontario at the time, went on a hunger strike after asking for a meeting about Treaties. I remember her standing up at a microphone the day she declared she would go on a hunger strike. It was right after a presentation about the plight of people from Lake St. Martin, Manitoba who were flooded from their communities a year before and still didn't know if they'd be able to go home. Most of their homes were destroyed and the land they lived on was not habitable. Still, the Manitoba and federal governments didn't seem to be in any rush to get them home. Instead, the people were suffering from several things while living in Winnipeg. Chief Spence took exception to that and talked about her community's experiences with being disrespected by governments in their own lands.

The National Chief, encouraged by Chiefs from across Canada, wrote a letter to Prime Minister Harper and the Governor General inviting them to meet with the Chiefs at the Delta Hotel in downtown Ottawa to discuss Treaty and greater respect for Indigenous people. I'm oversimplifying it, but in general Chiefs and grassroots people were calling out racism and racist policies and calling for greater input over their own lives. The Chiefs set a deadline for how long they were going to wait, but the deadline came and went. The Prime Minister's office told the Chiefs they weren't attending the meeting and wanted to meet certain Chiefs at their own offices.

The Chiefs doubled down on their messages to meet at their own terms with the PM and GG via media. They were going to wait until eleven a.m. that day, and if he didn't show up, they were going to march on the streets. In the Manitoba delegation room, I was with Chiefs, Councillors, Elders, and several others, including my boss, Grand Chief Nepinak.

Once the clock struck eleven, a Berens River Band Councillor and lawyer, Joan Jack, stood up and said, "That's it, let's go. Sheila, you lead the way." Meaning me! I was on my phone when I heard her, in constant communication with members of the media, giving them updates on what was happening. I wasn't expecting to be called on to lead the group out of the room and out of the building onto the street.

But there I was. I stood up and walked toward the door of the one of the meeting rooms on the second floor at the Delta Hotel, not really knowing where I was going just yet. As I did, everyone in the room lined up behind me. I stepped out of the room as other delegations from the other rooms started opening their doors and started walking with us. We became a massive crowd very quickly. We walked down the stairs, into the main meeting room the delegates had gathered in the day before and the crowd got even bigger. I headed toward the front door of the hotel and outside. Once outside, I didn't actually know which way to go! I had to ask a doorman which way Parliament Hill was; he pointed and I walked. So did the crowd of about three hundred, chanting! One of the Chiefs eventually helped me guide the crowd. He's experienced with horses, and it seemed like he was trying to herd a team of them as he yelled and whistled to get people's attention. I was glad to get his help because we were on the street by now, in traffic with drivers honking their horns, clearly confused and likely annoyed that our group was interrupting their drive. The feeling of overwhelming strength showed up in goosebumps all over my arms every once in a while. It was an incredible sight.

I can still see the pictures in my mind and you can easily find some of the pictures from this time on the internet. Hundreds if not thousands of us walking under a heavy snowfall, chanting 'Idle No More,' for example, walking together as some with drums sang songs. Thankfully, the Hill wasn't too far away, and we made it there just as another massive crowd of mostly grassroots protestors and activists from the INM movement also joined the rally. The rally was massive. Invigorating. Joan Jack was seen on TV that day scolding former AFN National Chief Matthew Coon Come for going in to meet the PM instead of demanding he meet with all the Chiefs. We saw Matthew as he was walking in, and Joan and others asked him to not go in. He simply answered, without looking at us, "I'm going in for my people."

"I know your mom and I'm going to tell her what you're doing," yelled back Joan.

We all laughed, a perfect example of how Indigenous people use humour when there's nothing else to do in highly stressful situations. Through tears of disappointment in seeing Matthew going in—disappointed because I had held him in high regard since I had worked on his campaign just years before to get him elected as the AFN National Chief—I had a good laugh too! It was a much-needed lighthearted moment for all of us there.

There were months of INM rallies and events across Canada at that time and the movement inspired the 'Rock the Vote' movement where organizers encouraged Indigenous people to get involved with the upcoming federal election. Some say, and I agree, that the Indigenous vote made a difference in that election driven by the desire to get the Harper government out and a new one in.

As the federal election campaigns started, it seemed that the INM movement started to slow down some, but the calls for an MMIW Inquiry continued as more bodies were discovered and people were still going missing. Sadly, it wasn't until after the body of fifteen-year-old Tina Fontaine was found in August 2014 in the Red River in downtown

Winnipeg that the calls for an inquiry were galvanized. Average Winnipeggers and Canadians were shocked to learn the girl's tiny body was found wrapped in a carpet and purposely dumped in the murky water of the Red River. That's when we saw about a thousand diverse faces join a memorial walk in Tina's honour that led to the Alexander Docks where Tina was found. This was the same dock my high school friends Doug and Dave used to fish off of. I went with them once and remembered that site very well.

At the time of the discovery, the police were actually looking for the body of Faron Hall, a man who was known as the Homeless Hero. He was seen jumping off a bridge and police were in the water searching for him when they came across Tina's body.

Faron was a Dakota man from Dakota Tipi First Nation in Manitoba. I was introduced to him while I was still reporting at CBC. In May 2009, witnesses saw him jump in the rushing and swollen Red River to save a teen he saw falling into the river. I didn't believe the woman who initially told me the story. She told me a homeless man jumped in and pulled a boy out of the river. When I dug more, I coincidentally knew one of the witnesses who'd talked to Faron after the incident and who has become one of Winnipeg's biggest homeless persons' advocates, Marion Willis. When I reached Marion to ask about the rescue, she confirmed yes, the only one who jumped in to save the flailing teen was the seemingly homeless man.

We went down to the river where it happened so I could interview her and get her story about what she saw. Again, coincidentally, Faron was still near the spot, which was where he and his friends hung out. It was kind of their living room. I talked to him, and he agreed to tell me his story on camera. We all marveled at his bravery, and it turns out that the rest of Canada did as well. After telling his story that night as the lead and exclusive story, the rest of the media outlets started chasing down Faron and his friends to get the story. Within a few days, Faron was a celebrity, going on national news programs. Winnipeg's then-mayor, Sam Katz, met with Faron and gave him gifts, hailing him a hero.

About five months after his first river rescue, Faron saved one of his friends from drowning. He was trying to save two men who went into the river to cool off on a hot summer day. These friends lost control and Faron tried to help them out but could only help one and the other friend drowned.

I became friends with Faron during our first interview. He would stop in at CBC to visit me and once in a while I'd run into him on the street and we'd chat. For a few years after the initial story, for which I received a Gemini Award nomination and won an RTNDA award, we maintained our friendship. I saw him struggle to get back to living in an apartment as he felt uncomfortable leaving his friends outside while he slept inside.

He also had problems with alcoholism that stemmed from his childhood experiences. He was a good man who protected his friends. He was a leader to them on the street, and I saw how his friends revered him. I think he sometimes saw this as a lot of pressure because he didn't like letting people down. I don't know why or how he ended up on the bridge and jumping off to his death, but I believe it was his last act of heroism because Tina's body was found while they were searching for him. Faron will always be a hero to me and many others.

At the Red River, Tina Fontaine, who was from Sagkeeng First Nation in northeastern Manitoba, also became a hero. Sadly, because of her life and how she died, she inspired the nation and the world to pay closer attention to the issue of MMIW. It seemed that people were starting to finally understand what a national tragedy this actually was and is. The other sad reality about Tina is that she died at the hands of the systems that should have protected her.

Tina was a ward of Manitoba's Child Welfare system. She had family, in particular, one great-aunt and uncle, Thelma and Joseph Favel, who had her in their care for most of her life. But according to family, as she got older, like many children in care, she wanted to see her biological mother in Winnipeg after not seeing her for years. Her father, a residential school survivor, was killed about three years prior to Tina's murder.

According to a report released in March 2019 by the Manitoba's Advocate for Children and Youth, Tina's Great-Aunt Thelma had tried desperately to get counselling and other supports for Tina before she died but couldn't get the help she'd hoped to get for the teen. The report talks about the fact that Tina struggled from the effects of colonization and the Indian Residential School era. Her late father was a survivor who ended up struggling with addictions and was in trouble with the law because of the violence he displayed. Her mother had been a ward of the child welfare system herself and became a teen mom who also struggled with addictions and being subjected to violence and sexual exploitation at the hands of Tina's father. Nevertheless, Tina mattered a great deal to her family, and they tried to get her help she needed to address the pain she and her siblings were carrying from their and their parents' life experiences.

Tina wanted what almost all of us want in life, a good life, as described by her aunt who helped raise her. According to facts brought out during a trial against a man initially charged with her murder, she came into contact with Winnipeg Police and health officials at a Winnipeg hospital before her body was found. She arrived in Winnipeg in June 2014, just over a month before she died, trying to reconnect with her mother who she hadn't seen for years. She was only supposed to stay about a week for the visit, but problems started and she ended up on the streets until social workers placed her in hotels for care. While she was placed at hotels, she started running away and was reported missing at least four times in the few weeks she was in Winnipeg. She also ended up at an emergency room after passersby found her in a parking lot, sleeping and possibly having been sexually assaulted. She was eventually discharged, and a social worker placed her in a hotel with a respite worker who couldn't convince Tina to stay and rest. She ended up back on the street. One of the people she spent time with was an older man who was eventually charged and acquitted for her death. According to reports, this man exploited Tina and gave her drugs and alcohol. In days leading up to Tina's death, she was considered missing, and Winnipeg police officers came across her in a car with a much older man. The officers were concerned but ultimately let the pair go. Family and friends wonder why police didn't question the man further that night and why they didn't take the teenager to safety.

There are many other sad facts about Tina's case, very similar to thousands of other cases across the country that are part of the national tragedy of MMIW. After the man accused was acquitted, he was set free—there wasn't a strong enough case to prove he killed her. We were all devastated, especially her family and friends, of course. As we left the courtroom with Thelma and other family members, Thelma had to sit back down on a bench in the hallway of the courthouse. She was feeling weak. I stopped to talk to her to see how she was feeling. When I looked into her eyes, I felt like I was standing in a dry desert on a windy day. I staggered for a second, feeling what I think was part of the tremendous weight Thelma and others were feeling. I asked her if she still wanted to talk to the media. She knew the media wanted to hear from her, but she said she just couldn't do it that day. She had been so strong in sharing Tina's and her own story, but the day of the verdict was too much. I asked her what message I and others who were there should deliver. She asked for calm, she said she didn't want to see any more violence. This was also just after another teen, Colten Boushie, was fatally shot on a Saskatchewan farm. He and his friends had been looking for help with a flat tire when the farmer they came across pulled out a gun, trying to scare them off and accusing them of being up to no good. The man shot Colten but was acquitted of the teen's death.

Tensions were again high during that time and many people were ready to revolt at the news of both tragedies. By this time, I had left AMC and was working for another media outlet, CTV. I was then approached to run for the position of the MKO Grand Chief. Raymond Cormier was charged for Tina's death in December 2015, three months after I was elected Grand Chief. He was acquitted about three years later, six months before my term ended in 2018. The MMIW inquiry was announced by the new Liberal government months after they got into power in October 2015 and the commission and commissioners began their work in September 2016.

Right after the trial in 2018 though, I and other leaders, stood in place of Tina's great-aunt Thelma in front of the Winnipeg courthouse, demanding justice. We also passed on the message that Thelma was calling for calm and peace, not retaliation. I remember saying among other things, "This is not the outcome anybody wanted. The systems, everything that got involved in Tina's life, failed her. We've all failed her. We as a nation need to do better for our young people" to the media and MMIW supporters who stood with us. I felt at times like that—we could've done more to avoid the tragedy. But I also wanted average Canadians to take responsibility for her death. I felt so strongly that we needed to approach it that way, to recruit more allies in helping to end the violence against Indigenous people.

Chapter 22

BLOOD MEMORY

The moment I realized I was an MMIW survivor was when I went to my first vigil in the outskirts of Winnipeg in August 2007. A teen girl, who had been missing for some time, was found dead next to a tree. Her family had invited the public and media to join them in a vigil where she was found. I attended the vigil with a seasoned reporter while I was just starting out. I was still a casual reporter then and was still struggling to find my place as a storyteller. That day, my colleague Donna Carriero was assigned to cover the vigil and do a live hit from there. I went on my own because it wasn't part of my duties at the time. But I wanted to know what was going on. Being there, seeing all the pain on the family's faces and hearing the cries had an incredible impact on me, an impact that hasn't left me since that day. I wondered how it was possible that a young girl in Winnipeg could be left to die the way she did.

I left the vigil that night unable to think about anything else for a while. It's when I started listening and paying attention to similar stories other families were telling. But at the time I still didn't really know what to do about any of that myself. The stories resonated with me, but I didn't know how to approach them as a reporter. I think I was trying to reconcile what was happening at the same time, trying to understand why the stories sounded so familiar to me. But I was definitely opening myself to hear more of these stories and experiences.

The stories I heard were similar to some experiences I lived through in high school: being introduced to older men by a friend, being introduced to a type of brothel and trying to fit it in, not knowing I was actually in danger. The bawdy house was very close to my school near downtown Winnipeg in the West End, a multicultural neighbourhood with modest homes and lower incomes and which has one of the higher crime rates in the city. When I went to high school there, there were plenty of places to eat for little money and the neighbourhood had one of the most popular roller rinks in the city. The bawdy house was just a few blocks from the roller rink. A house that wasn't a home: it looked like one from the outside but inside it was a cold dark place where older men looked at younger women as property.

I was super shy and barely talked to anyone then and I certainly wasn't assertive yet. But I knew I didn't want to go in the house or anywhere in it with the man who wanted to know my name, but I did. This man was in his forties and I was fifteen years old. I was brought back then to the time the predator in my childhood neighbourhood would take advantage of my innocence. But this time I felt an immense feeling of strength, and I got up and left the room before he could get any further under my clothes. I walked straight to my friend and said I had to go. She agreed and we left and went back to school. I did go back to the bawdy house several times with her because she was my friend and I liked hanging out with her. But she knew I didn't want to so most of the time we'd only go quickly and leave even though the guys inside tried to make us stay. I must've been annoying, wasting everyone's time.

One of the stories I heard from people I met in my early days of reporting was about brothels like the one I knew of. But the stories I was told were of young girls, who were mostly Indigenous, who stayed and ended up becoming really intoxicated and/or drugged. These girls would then be passed around by the adult men, from room to room like objects. I saw a glimpse of this once, and it scared me enough to never want to go there again.

Thankfully, I was able to make it out of those situations. I know it was only because my parents and grandparents prayed for me. I felt it. I know I'm fortunate to have had strong connections to my parents and grandparents as I grew up, I believe it made a huge difference in my life. I know many Indigenous people who've been cut off from their biological families through colonization and have had a harder life because of the disconnect. As a result, not everyone made it out of the hands of predators and harm's way. In an attempt to assimilate Indigenous Peoples, government regulations severed family ties for many Indigenous families.

The racist policies then made many people vulnerable by stripping away their sense of purpose, confidence, and hope. The feelings of disparity were then passed from generation to generation. So not everyone has had people to pray for them or help in other ways through life, making them vulnerable and easy targets for predators to take advantage of. Some of the predators ended up being friends of friends, like the one I had who recruited other girls for the men in the brothels. But I believe my friend, who was also a teenager, was vulnerable as well.

The experiences of being a vulnerable teenager came flooding back when I started as a reporter. At that time, media were still calling the victims prostitutes, street workers, or hookers. That practice stems from racist and misogynistic views that were and still are a result of institutional racism. Inadvertently or not, the media and society blamed the victims for their own deaths, disappearances, and hard lives. It was almost a free pass for Canadians to not care about these women and girls because they were viewed as being 'morally corrupt'—implying women and girls chose the lifestyles they were in, so it was their problem.

The disdain for Indigenous people that was carried on by blood memory and flowed from generation to generation also gave police and social agencies less motivation to stop the crimes against women and girls. And rarely, if at all, did the media or society talk about the perpetrators. Not even to this day. You'll rarely hear any stories about predators and yet you'll be told about every sordid detail of a victim's struggles and any criminal record, no matter how minor, they may have had. This was the case for Tina Fontaine in 2014 and is still normal today.

It's not lost on me and many others that these problems exist and persist mostly towards Indigenous women, girls, and two-spirited people. Why? Because of the disregard and disdain against Indigenous people that Canadians have been trained to accept. Yes, of course, non-Indigenous people from other cultural groups have had their own problems and some similar ones, but the disrespect for Indigenous people seems commonplace in Canada and the most vulnerable have been women, girls, and two-spirited people.

But back in 2005, families and friends started pushing back at the media, saying they'd only talk to the media if they told the stories of victims with their names and roles in their families—that they were sisters, moms, aunties, or daughters. That they were loved, missed, and deserved to be protected. It was becoming impossible for the media to tell stories about MMIW any other way.

A decade after I witnessed the rise of the MMIW champions, our world was in a much different place. Of course, the struggle and fight to end all forms of violence against Indigenous women and girls is still an issue—for all Indigenous people actually, but women and girls are disproportionately impacted by violence. Some Elders say the violence and disrespect of women and girls began as soon as explorers made it on the shores of North America, but it was in that ten-year period I witnessed for myself the strength and resilience of our women, girls, and allies. During that time, I met one particular family who challenged me to dig deeper into the stories of MMIW when they told me the story of Cherisse Houle as they knew it.

It was the late Cherisse's story that inspired me to co-produce a film about the issue. Our film, *1200+* talks about the history of Indigenous people in Canada and some of the leading causes of the epidemic of MMIW. My film partner, Leonard Yakir, and I met at the Alexander Docks on the Red River in Winnipeg, near where Tina Fontaine's body was discovered. I was there working as a reporter; he was there taking pictures of the area. He's from Winnipeg but lives in the States and was in town for family matters.

Leonard's wife, Susan, and my cameraman started talking about Tina's case and their conversation inevitably involved Leonard and me. Leonard said he was a filmmaker and was interested in learning more about the issue of MMIW. I told him I was interested in making a film about the topic and we exchanged contact information to talk about a possible project.

Within weeks Leonard and I talked about making a film; he came back to Winnipeg and we started filming. We didn't really have an idea about the length, exact content, or title of our film. We started with a diary written by the last foster mother of the late Cherisse Houle. In it she documented the teenager's comings and goings for about a year. She listed all the places the foster parents picked her up and the dealings they had with the child welfare workers who placed Cherisse with them.

Initially, the foster mom shared the diary with me when I was still reporting for CBC after interviewing her about Cherisse, days after her body was discovered in a creek just outside Winnipeg city limits on July 1st, 2009. Within two weeks of Cherisse's death, two other teen girls' bodies were also found just outside Winnipeg. It was a scary time for many of us in the Indigenous community, not knowing what was going on, wondering if there was a serial killer targeting young Indigenous women. After the discovery of the three girls' bodies, activists called for a task force to be called, looking into the deaths of the three girls and others who were killed. The number of cases of dead or missing Indigenous women and girls across the country was growing every day.

To this day, however, the cases involving Cherisse Houle and Hilary Angel Wilson, whose bodies were found within two weeks of each other, both in the outskirts of Winnipeg, have not been solved. No one has been arrested or charged with their deaths. In fact, very few of the over 1,200 cases across Canada have been solved. In our documentary, we talk about the possibility of serial killers, we talk about the link to the Indian Residential School era, colonization, and some of the police responses to the cases. We tried very hard not to come up with conclusions for viewers, but most people who watch the film now question why police haven't done more or been held accountable for not solving most cases, even after a police task force was set up.

When I was first given the foster mom's diary of the last year of Cherisse's life, the foster mom told me that she tried to hand it over to Winnipeg Police first but no one investigating the case ever accepted it. Again, one of the main complaints I've received when I would interview families and survivors of MMIW, was that when they tried to report cases to police, officers were often condescending or just didn't believe the person trying to report a case. It's no wonder that there are persisting trust issues between police and Indigenous people in this country, yes, with other people of colour too. Our country and all Canadians have learned the same racist views from generation to generation, creating systemic and institutional racism everywhere. To hear Cherisse's foster mom tell me that investigators weren't interested in even seeing her diary, reminded me of the willful ignorance I heard about over and over again.

It wasn't until I did a news story about the diary and held it up as I was talking that the police took momentary interest in it. Cherisse's foster mom called me right after the story aired and asked me to make a copy of it and bring back the original so police could have it. I did. But when an investigator showed up to see it, he took just a few seconds and flipped through it, dismissed it, and left, saying there was nothing in it they could use. Yet it was filled with many names and phone numbers of people who were in contact with Cherisse in her last year and places she was at. All of the information in it was still recent and most of the numbers I found and called still worked. One particular number I called was a man's number that showed up on the call list several times. A woman answered and I asked for the man. She asked me why and I said I was a journalist working on a story about Cherisse Houle. She said, "That's my husband, but what does he have to do with her?" I didn't want to make any speculations to her, so I just asked her to have him call me back. He didn't. But of course, as a journalist I could only do so much with all that information.

While shooting our film, I presented the Winnipeg Police Chief of the day, Danny Smyth, the diary, and he accepted it. However, by then, seven years after it was written, I'm sure the leads in it were cold. What I was able to find out in my reporting and working on the documentary is that she was close friends with another young girl who died in a similar way to Cherisse and similar to the way Fonessa Bruyere had died two summers before Cherisse and Hilary. Cherisse and Hilary's bodies were found within two weeks of each other. They also had common friends, men who were part of a gang who procured young Indigenous girls for sex. From the stories the families and friends told me after the gruesome discoveries, it sounded like the same type of gangs I encountered when I was a teen. The men I encountered were from Southeast Asian countries who immigrated to Canada for jobs and a better life. In doing research for *1200+*, we learned that eventually some of the men from these gangs were arrested for other crimes, given short sentences, and deported back to their countries.

What I also learned about Cherisse was that she was a new mom when she died, she wanted to be with her family, she was loving and funny, and she had lived in ninety-two foster homes in her short seventeen-year life. Her biological mom and sister told us their family struggled after her mom and father's relationship broke down. Mom is a residential school survivor and saw and felt the effects of colonization her whole life. So did Cherisse and her sister Jessica. In fact, many people who struggle with addictions, homelessness, and other social ills have being placed in the foster care system in common. Some who study the effects of colonization say the Residential School, Day School and Sixties Scoop eras damaged people and now the child welfare system is doing the same. In Manitoba alone, there are over 10,000 children in care and about 90 percent of kids in care are Indigenous.

Sadly, Cherisse's story is just one of thousands of stories that we tried to capture in the film. There have been many more stories and lives lost since then. The problem persists and, in my view, MMIW is a national tragedy, an epidemic, a societal problem.

In spite of the challenges and pain associated with MMIW though, I also saw one of the greatest victories of MMIW when I had the honour of seeing the issue highlighted at a United Nations forum on the Status of Women in New York where I was invited to speak. I even had an opportunity to screen our film during the forum. I attended the same annual forum for two years and what I learned while I was there was that we from Canada were the leaders on the topic of MMIW around the world. Women from all over the world were asking us how we made the topic so well-known and how it became a national election issue. I told them the stories of the MMIW champions and their relentless efforts to raise awareness about the issue that led to many changes in Canada.

But even as the awareness is being raised, the number of victims just keeps rising. And more people get away with the disappearances and deaths while the police don't seem to be in any hurry to solve the cases even as the Canadian public and government start to pay more attention to the stories. One of the greatest challenges I see to putting an end to MMIW is that many Indigenous women and girls are kept in a vulnerable state through economic starvation that withholds from them the dignity they deserve.

Withholding proper resources for good educational systems, health care, and job opportunities are just a few ways I see the starvation is happening. And it's been happening since the Indian Act was imposed in 1876. All the social determinants of health such as housing, access to clean water, mental health support and the like also show the lack of respect for the Original People of these lands. Because of high levels of poverty and poor health conditions, many Indigenous people, both on and off reserve, have few opportunities to become self-sufficient as they once were before colonization, creating another generational curse, the economic starvation kind. People can't create a 'nest egg' for their children or grandchildren to help them get a good start, some can't even meet day-to-day needs let alone put money away for anything else. That's why many Indigenous advocates talk about 'Economic Reconciliation,' changing the way the systems are set up now, so Indigenous people can have a fair shake at life. How can we expect more from people when we don't support their rights to have their basic needs met?

Elders tell us as Indigenous people of a time when women had leadership roles in our communities, our families, our world. Author Arden Ogg reminds us that iskwewak, the Cree word for woman, comes from fire and heart. The fire and heart of our people are women, and if they suffer an entire nation suffers. Women took care of us as people, they delegated roles and responsibilities, they made decisions that best suited our nations. Women and girls were revered and protected. We see less of that now, and new attitudes toward Indigenous women and girls has its roots in colonization when settlers first started arriving in North America. Some storytellers say that the explorers who ended up on our shores didn't want to deal with the women when they first met the Original People of the lands now known as Canada. So, they didn't, and it seems since then, women, girls and those with gender fluidity have been pushed aside and marginalized.

Growing up learning about the Bible makes me appreciate the teachings in it and I still adhere to many of them, but I don't believe it was meant to change Indigenous people and how we are as nations of people. I believe we as Original People of these lands already had a relationship with the Creator, and I believe the teachings our people were born with are still valid and beautiful, including that women should be revered not hated or used. I also don't believe all men or boys disrespect women, but sadly some were taught that, and that keeps women, girls, and two-spirited people vulnerable. We all need to unlearn many things and start removing the mindsets that keep us separated and marginalized.

As a child, a teenager, and a young mom, I feel like I survived becoming an MMIW statistic. I lived under the fear of MMIW for half of my life, but the moment I realized I was a survivor, I moved to become a thriver and advocate. I became inspired to work in ending the epidemic almost every day of my life since—it's become a lifelong mission for me. The beauty of being a survivor is being able to connect with other survivors who have also become thrivers. Many of these people have gone on to do amazing things, and with all of their achievements, you may never know they are survivors and thrivers. You may never know what they've overcome to be where they're at. But the fact remains that the strength, the honour Indigenous women and girls—all Indigenous people—possess will not be contained. We have caught on to what's going on and to the attacks on our people. We are moving forward to change the course, to create a better path for future generations —for all of our future generations.

Chapter 23

ACTIVIST TO LEADER

In 2013, the Harper Government started retaliating against Indigenous people in response to the rallying cries by grassroots people and organizations. It started sending notices of massive funding cuts to mostly Indigenous political organizations across the country. The biggest cuts were to the Assembly of Manitoba Chiefs with an 80 percent reduction of funds. Coincidently, the AMC and Grand Chief Nepinak were among the most critical voices against the Harper Government in the media just before the cuts were imposed. Many people at the organizations had to either take pay cuts or find other jobs after that, and programs and resources were severely hampered.

The position I had as AMC's Chief Communications Officer was also heavily reduced to working about minimum wage. Meanwhile, I still had my family to support. I decided to leave AMC to work as a journalist again, this time at CTV. But I remember how hard it was to not think like an advocate and go back to being a neutral journalist. It wasn't impossible, but it was a transition that I needed to remind myself of almost daily.

I was able to tell some really important stories from CTV in my eighteen months there, and I met some incredible people who I'm still friends with today. I learned a lot about the world from there as well, though I think my activist brain was always on during story meetings and even in the final stories I told. I still told balanced stories, but I struggled not to share my own opinions.

Then one day as I was gathering interviews for a story, I got a call from my friend Jennifer Wood that changed my trajectory once again. "I have a great idea," she said. "You should run to become the next MKO Grand Chief." She was referring to the Manitoba Keewatinowi Okimakanak, the Indigenous political organization that then represented thirty Cree, Dene, and Oji-Cree communities. I think I choked on my sip of coffee when she uttered those words! We chatted further, and I think I said I'd have to think about it. But honestly, I think I had a good laugh with my cameraman when we ended the call. The idea was foreign to me, mostly because I just finished my role as a communications director for another Grand Chief. I saw the hardships Chiefs, Councillors, their supporters, and other people went through to advocate for their rights and place in this country.

I wasn't sure if I was able to carry that load, or if I even should. I wondered what I had to offer, after all, I was just a reporter. Yes, I did work with Chiefs for a short time, but becoming one myself wasn't one of my life-long dreams. I admired our leaders and I supported their work, but I didn't see myself as a leader. Except with my children, at home, and in media, I suppose.

However, I did get a taste of an official leadership role once before becoming the MKO Grand Chief. I ran for and won by acclamation the position of Vice President for the Native Student Association at Assiniboine Community College in Brandon, Manitoba in 1995. I got in by acclamation because no one else wanted to run! I remember the biggest reason for stepping up was to see if I could help improve student life. I guess that was a glimpse of my role as an advocate coming out, but I didn't see it like that back then, even though I was taking courses in a program that taught me to be a better global citizen. During that time, I was taught that in order to make the world a better place you must be willing to help and be bold. I was still in survival mode. Yet, even while living in an abusive relationship, I stepped up.

Being a student VP had several challenges, mostly around managing all the duties I had at home and the coursework I needed to get done. But having the extra duties helped me gain self-confidence. That was when I first started noticing I was able to gather myself and find enough strength to eventually leave my first husband for good. By helping others, I was helping myself. Though I didn't realize at the time that that's what I was doing, I saw my role then as setting goals to help my fellow students' concerns get addressed. I also don't remember doing anything really cool or amazing as a VP, except managing to bring in the then-Assembly of Manitoba Chiefs, Grand Chief Phil Fontaine, to speak at our college!

I impressed myself and others when that happened. The whole college was abuzz, and it even gained a bit of local media coverage. The biggest thing I remember Mr. Fontaine saying at that time is that Native people can and should run our own affairs. That notion was very familiar to me because my late father used to say the same thing. Coincidently, Mr. Fontaine and my dad were colleagues once at a place called Manitoba Indian Brotherhood before it transitioned into AMC.

In hosting Mr. Fontaine back then, I would have asked more questions if I had an idea that twenty years later I'd become a Grand Chief myself someday! The first female Grand Chief of the Manitoba Keewatinowi Okimakanak, no less. Before that happened though, I had to lead myself and my kids away from domestic violence. I had to figure out what my actual dreams were and a way to pursue them. I also had to figure out how I was going to raise my children the way my parents did, with a mother and a father. I ended up doing all that before I realized my lifelong dream of becoming a journalist, and long before I was recruited for leadership.

During the lead up to becoming a Grand Chief I had many teachable moments linked to my parents and their teachings. Each time I ran into a challenge, I remembered pieces of advice my dad, the former Chief who became a lifelong leader, gave me. The main one was to not let what anyone with negative attitudes and words said touch my heart, not to take anything personally. To think past them and not to let them influence my decisions or actions and not to say anything back when people attacked me personally. I still struggle with that teaching sometimes, but it's how I try to live and work.

As more people started asking me to run, I turned to my parents for advice. I also reached out to other friends, colleagues, and every Elder I came across, asking them what they thought. I think I was looking for someone to say no, it's not a good idea. The only one I asked for advice who suggested I stay in media was Murray Sinclair when he was still the Lead Commissioner of the Truth and Reconciliation Commission. He said I was needed more in media. I took that to heart and wanted to comply, but the calls to run started to get louder and louder.

My parents immediately said yes and prayed with me. Other Elders I spoke to were very clear that they wanted me to run. The one conversation I remember the most is from a councillor, Marilyn Wood, from the Garden Hill First Nation. She wasn't a senior yet, but she carried herself and spoke in a way that wise elders do. Always ready to give advice, she certainly gave me a stern response when I asked her what she thought of the idea. "Run," she said. "What are you waiting for, go. And don't consider it a privilege or compliment you're being asked, this is your responsibility," she added. When she said that, all the hesitation I was feeling left me and I decided to run.

But I only knew how to help in a campaign, not *be* the campaign, so I turned to my good friends Jennifer and Darcy, who had recruited and trained me for other campaigns, to lead the way. Our MKO campaign lasted only three months, but we were busy the whole time travelling all over the North and back south to meetings with the leaders we needed to meet.

I met many smart people who knew how to strategize, and together we began to implement the ideas and strategies we came up with. I was the one at the podiums talking to people, but there were many people with me who helped me stay on track. My work as a journalist also helped me because I wasn't afraid to speak in public or to the media. I was also skilled in being brief or expanding messages when I needed to.

But one thing I learned quickly about leadership is that most leaders never really lead alone. Whether they acknowledge those around them or not, leadership is actually a team effort. Fortunately for me, I always had people around me who had the best interest of others at heart. I can't say everyone I led with were always loyal but even they contributed to the best work I was fortunate enough to do. There were wins and losses, but the constant is, I never felt like a lone wolf!

Chapter 24

LEADING LIKE A WOMAN

Playing games as a child like duck-duck-goose was fun. I liked that it was easy to follow and that I didn't have to lead all the time. But as an adult life got complicated, and when I had to follow others in order to live, I became a more conscious and active follower and leader. Thankfully, there were several amazing role models who were leaders themselves in my life and I was more than happy to play a supportive role when I needed to, including my time as a journalist when I had to follow the lead of camera technicians, producers, or editors. Another time of course, was in my work as the communications director for one of the most influential leaders in Canada at that time. I had to pay attention to everything going on inside and outside the office, while carefully following, and at times guiding, the direction the Grand Chief needed to go, especially when it came to sensitive topics like MMIW and other issues that impacted people's personal lives.

But outside of my parents, the leaders I admired the most and followed are the ones without official titles, including one of my closest friends and colleagues, Jennifer Wood. She and her husband Darcy took me under their wings and taught me almost everything I know about Indigenous politics. Some things I had to learn myself!

As you know already from previous chapters, Jennifer and Darcy have became constants in my life since I met them in 1997 when I was in one of the biggest transitions in my life. But Jennifer and I were connected long before I met her. She is originally from a reserve in southern Ontario, Neyaashiinigmiing. Coincidentally though, she moved with her dad and stepmother as a teenager to my home reserve, Bunibonibee, a year before I was born. Her stepmother was posted in Bunibonibee as a United Church minister. They lived there until Jennifer was sent to live at the same residence for residential school my mom was sent to a few years earlier in Portage la Prairie, Manitoba. But she met my parents and my other relatives while she was there.

As life went on from there for her, Jennifer eventually became a skilled event planner and one of top Indigenous political strategists in Canada. She and Darcy met at the school in Portage la Prairie. This dynamic duo ended up working with Elijah Harper, one of the most influential Indigenous leaders in Canada since the early '90s. Her first official job in politics was working for the late Elijah Harper after that famous moment when he said, "No," to the Meech Lake Accord while he was an MLA for northern Manitoba. The same Elijah Harper who visited our house when I was a little girl, while he was on a campaign trail to become the MLA. My late father knew him more than I did, of course, because they were colleagues as Chiefs before. But it was much later that Jennifer and I realized how connected we were on several significant levels.

There are likely very few people you'll meet in life where you feel God, Creator has ordained a friendship. I would say the friendship I have with Jennifer and Darcy is one of those. Evidence, to me, is the fact that four decades after Jennifer left my home reserve, she and I ended up working together on historic campaigns including ones for Phil Fontaine, Matthew Coon Come, and myself in 2015 for the MKO election and again in 2018 for the AFN election for National Chief and as a candidate for the AMC election in 2021.

The work for me as a leader was tough in many ways, and what happened just minutes before I was declared the new and first female MKO Grand Chief was a quick lesson in how challenging the role would be when another candidate knelt in front of me, thinking I had lost to him because I am a woman! The work I chose to walk into was challenging enough, but also doing it as a woman became an issue for some. The fact I am a woman only came up a few times during the short campaign, once when a journalist brought it up and one of the other candidates kept mentioning it. The same one, the man I beat in the election. Did I say I beat him in the election yet?!

Aside from the election drama in 2015, it was quite an achievement for MKO Chiefs and Councillors to elect their first female Grand Chief and people were excited. Of course, so was I, as were my team and my family. It turned out that being a female Grand Chief was a big deal. Mostly positive. In the first year I was reminded almost all the time that people I met were happy to know how we managed to make it happen. I will say it wasn't my goal to be the first female GC, but it did feel good, especially since there weren't many of us across the country. There are more and more female Chiefs but certainly not as many as there should be.

After I was declared the new Grand Chief, almost immediately there was a Pipe Ceremony to bless the occasion. We as delegates were invited to sit in a circle as an Elder and his helper led us through prayers, lifting up the pipe and passing it around the circle for everyone to partake. I had to decline because I was on my moon time, my period. Women and girls who are on their period are typically not allowed to participate fully in spiritual ceremonies because anyone on their time is said to be 'too powerful'—powerful enough to interfere or draw away spiritual powers from a Pipe Ceremony, sweat lodge or Sundance. Spiritual leaders have said if women or girls participate in any of those ceremonies while they're on their moon time, someone in the circle could get sick from it. To avoid that, anyone on their period is asked to voluntarily disclose that they're on their time and avoid participating. As it is, women and girls are asked to wear long skirts in any of those ceremonies, even if they don't have their period. Again, for the same reason, a female's power is too strong and needs to be contained. The other teaching I've been told by my people who follow Indigenous ways of spirituality is that a female's period is a way for her body to purify and recharge itself. The teachings draw similarities to the moon cycle, and once a month when there's a full moon the earth is affected by the ocean tides—a new moon signifies renewal.

These teachings are very different from the religious teachings I learned at home and church. I didn't learn much about my moon time but women on their period are seen as unclean. But the Bible doesn't say being on your period or being unclean is a sin. In fact, blood in the Bible is one of the powerful and sacred symbols in its teachings. Blood is associated with atonement in the scriptures, including the shedding of it, as Jesus did on the Cross.

There are of course other teachings about periods from other beliefs. But for me, what resonated about having a period is that it's meant as protection for my body and spirit. I complained about having my period once while on one of our campaign trails, and Jennifer told me not to think badly of it but to think of it as coming to protect me. I felt empowered when she said that and ever since then I've valued being on my moon time. And it couldn't have come at a better time than when I woke up on the morning of the MKO election on September 2, 2015. As soon as I woke up it was there, and I felt a sense of calm that it would be a good day no matter what. And it was an excellent day.

I believe all of the negative things that happened or were said during the day didn't have its normal effect on me because of my moon time. So, I embraced it and it seems almost every difficult day I faced during my time as leader, I was protected by my woman-ness. One of the women councillors who was at the MKO election came up to me after the Pipe Ceremony and said, "I'm so glad you won, it's the first time I felt comfortable being in a ceremony like that." In fact, I've heard similar sentiments from women and girls at other events since that day.

Of course, not everyone was happy to see a woman in the mostly circles of men at Chiefs or government tables. In one of my first meetings, a bureaucrat from Indigenous Services Canada didn't seem to feel comfortable with me there as the Grand Chief. I had one of my male support staff come with me to the meeting and the gentleman we met only wanted to address him, not me. Even when I asked him a question, he would look at my male assistant while he answered. I spoke up and made sure he knew he needed to address me. He caught on but it was the strangest thing to experience. It makes me wonder what it was like for women during the time when settlers first came to Turtle Island.

The misogyny and chauvinism weren't just from non-Indigenous men, however. One of the first male Chiefs I had to deal with in the first few months of being the Grand Chief didn't like the fact I made decisions about our organization and where I wanted to take it. He vehemently disagreed and worked to turn people against me. There are of course a few reasons behind his action. The first, and maybe the one that inspired all his other complaints, was me beating the candidate he wanted to win. In my first meeting with a small group of Chiefs, he walked out and it was clear he wasn't happy. In a follow-up meeting to address his concerns, he worked very hard to turn his fellow Chiefs against me, asking them to support his wishes to leave MKO as a group of Chiefs. The other chiefs didn't agree, and the meeting ended. As we all left, this particular Chief and I were the last to leave and instead of shaking my hand he motioned for me to sit on his lap and laughed.

I didn't know how to respond, partly because I didn't want to strain the relationship any further. Thankfully, one of the other Chiefs, a female Chief, saw him doing that and she reprimanded him right there. I left it at that, but this same Chief made his disdain and disrespect for me known throughout my whole time as the MKO Grand Chief. I still said hi to him whenever I saw him and shook his hand. He would never look at me and he got especially uncomfortable when his wife was with him and I'd chat her up. She is a nice woman and I didn't mind having a quick visit with her. He did not like that.

There are a few other times I saw male leaders displaying their sexist views. These leaders are leaders of larger Indigenous political organizations. During my bid to become the Grand Chief, one kept reminding me that he had a lot of influence over several electorates and it would be good to have his support. He was still a local chief of a Manitoba First Nation at the time, and he reminded me about his 'influence' when we were alone as he placed himself in front of me and tried to hold and kiss me. Thankfully, he was interrupted by a group of people who we heard coming up just as he maneuvered in. Being in that space with him reminded me of the time a molester took me into the woods as a very young child and attacked me. This same Chief has tried a few more times to get his way with me and has always tried reminding me of his influence. I told him once during one of these times that I was happily married, and he replied, "He doesn't need to know." I didn't agree or comply with his advances, at least not in the way he hoped for. I was nice to him and diverted his attention instead. Even today one of his tactics in any negotiations I've seen him in is to tell people who support him how 'influential' he is.

In another instance, when I asked the male leader of another large Indigenous organization why he didn't say hi when I saw him at a major event the day before, he replied, "I didn't see you there, but I saw you leave my hotel room at three this morning." He laughed, I didn't. I said, "You can't talk like that." He laughed some more and told me to relax while proceeding to tell me he had a resolution passed at his organization that hugs between men and women are allowed, that they're traditional. My professional relationship with him as a fellow leader soured greatly after that short encounter.

What's interesting about all of these incidents, and I know other leaders have witnessed them as well, is that some of the male leaders who are the biggest spokespeople for MMIW or other critical issues like that are the same ones who display this behaviour when they think no one is looking, or they display it to someone they think is not worthy of respect.

Traditionally, before colonization, it was women in Indigenous communities who were the leaders and delegators for their people. They were the spokespeople who looked after the people. I understand better why that is, because women and male leadership styles are different. Both are critically important for the health of our nations but different in important ways. For example—and a study done by advocate Sandra Deloronde confirms this—women lead with many people and goals in mind at once. Sometimes the process for women as they lead takes longer to achieve goals, but in the end, they are more inclusive and better for the long run. Male leaders are usually quick in making decisions and don't like to waste time in achieving a goal they see as the right one. Again, this type of leadership is important, especially in crisis situations but not always good when the end goal is not well thought out first.

Side note—I had someone ask me once what it was like to be a woman leader. I laughed and said, "I don't know. I was never a man, so I don't have another gender experience to compare it to, because I have never been a male leader!" We both laughed. But I do know, and I will always advise anyone who asks, to be true to yourself and run the way you were made. As women leaders it is easy to get pulled in to try and act like male leaders. In recent generations, we as Indigenous people have been taught to lead like men only. I say, if you're a woman—or maybe even a man—run like a woman, lead like a woman.

Don't get me wrong, I have always tried to give equal respect to male and female leaders, and leaders who identify as two-spirited people, because I expect the same. There are many great male, female and gender diverse leaders who are inclusive and respectful but there are not enough of them around right now, in my humble opinion. In fact, from what I've seen and experienced, women have been left out of leadership roles far too long, since colonization, when explorers landed on our shores, preferring to deal with men. Unfortunately, I could see how some men would've bought into that notion, because it gave them more power, especially over women, resources, and any decision making. And sadly, that same thinking still exists today. The only way I can see out of that, if we as Indigenous and non-Indigenous people are serious about restoring the balance of male and female leadership roles, is carving out spaces for only women to run for certain positions. For Indigenous political organizations, maybe that means that Grand Chief roles need to alternate between male and female leaders for a while until we are all comfortable in including and voting in women in these roles. I feel similar about mainstream politics—if the different parties are truly interested in 'Reconciliation' they should create or leave spaces for Indigenous candidates to run during elections. It's hard enough trying to fit Indigenous people in the Canadian political system as is and expect to succeed. Equally hard is trying to recruit Indigenous candidates and getting them to compete for electorates who don't always value them as people in the first place.

Let's have some election reforms, if we truly want that good life that we and our families aspire to: one of prosperity, health and happiness. We need to get back to a balanced environment where no one feels left out, but as long as we keep Indigenous women and girls out of Indigenous elections, we may never achieve what we all hope for. And as long as Indigenous people keep being disregarded, disrespected, and dispossessed in their own lands and left out of decision-making roles, we'll continue to see the hardships we see in Canada today. Let's all be brave. Period!

Chapter 25

#METOO

After I got going in my new role, a few more difficult people came into the picture to challenge me and my inner circle. One of the first was a woman who I genuinely have no idea why she grew to detest and challenge me. But she did and would go on social media to bash me, even though we had 'good conversations' before I was elected. When men are being misogynistic you kind of know what to expect, but when women are mean to other women, it feels worse for some reason. At least it does for me. The biggest or worst challenger I faced though, was the Chief I mentioned in the previous chapter who played up to my womanhood to degrade me.

The impression I get from this man is that he doesn't value women as leaders. When we were colleagues, I tolerated him making sexist remarks or jokes, but when I became a fellow leader, I was less tolerant and he realized it. To cope, he worked hard to undermine my role and tried several times to turn other leaders against me. When another female leader reprimanded him for making that sexual gesture to me, I chose to leave it there rather speaking publicly about it because I thought it would be easier for me to do my job as a Grand Chief. I decided that I had bigger issues to deal with and I didn't want other male leaders to feel uncomfortable with me. I did not want to be blacklisted as a woman or viewed as a woman some would say was too sensitive or rumoured to falsely accuse men just for my own gain. I had no issue with men flirting with me, especially since I became single a year after I got in as an elected leader—I am a woman after all! But what I couldn't accept was anyone who tried to gain anything over me just because I am a woman. And the difference between the two are very clear to me when I see it.

Still, I chose to internalize chauvinism to maintain the peace. Right or wrong that's what happened. And I think until we all get that level of respect we deserve as individuals, we'll see sexist behaviours continue. But speaking out about it in safe ways is also going to make a difference in the long run—I hope so anyway.

In the case with the Chief who tried to discredit me at every turn, I kept treating him with respect. In that case, I was thinking more about his wife, his family, and the people he represented. I felt that if they all believed in him, there must be something good about him. He was always unfriendly to me though, until he went too far and I had to remind him two years later about what he had done to me. I felt that I had no choice because he was getting to a point where he was moving past being disrespectful to me as an individual and starting to turn on MKO as an organization. I took exception to that because I believed we were doing important and necessary work for our people. I didn't agree with his complaints, and I had had enough of his underlying threats. I called and asked him to please be respectful of MKO, otherwise I'd have to talk openly about how he acted towards me, telling him he was one of the most disrespectful fellow Chiefs I'd worked with. For the most part he was civil to me after that, and he definitely changed his tone about MKO. And when the #MeToo movement burst onto the scene, I was reminded of the incidents I had experienced as a leader and in roles I had before that.

In two other workplaces I was in years prior to becoming Grand Chief, I let men I admired disrespect me to the point I became a conquest instead of a valued colleague. I feel I was doing great work and helped the 'companies' achieve new levels of greatness. I was extremely dedicated to the work in every job I've ever had, including the two workplaces where I was being actively pursued, simply for being a woman. These men in the two separate organizations were brilliant in their work, well known for their skills. I believed in them, and during those times I eventually felt I was neglecting my own family and my spouse to cater to the companies. I slowly started to let myself think that supporting these colleagues was more important than anything else. I felt like we did amazing work until the time they made their verbal advances physical. In both incidents, I walked away because I didn't want my complaints to hinder my chances for achievement or possibilities of advancement.

Walking away made me feel like shit. I left wondering what I had done for these powerful men think so poorly of me that they thought it was okay for them to prey on me.

I see this as part of a way that women get caught in traps. Not just women though. I know men have been caught in those kind predicaments as well where they have to choose between their dignity or their jobs. When it happened to me, it reminded me of when I was child and teenager being preyed upon by men seeking power and control. Feeling the same feeling as an adult, an accomplished adult even, doesn't make it any easier. In fact, I blamed myself again. When I was child, I thought I had my ponytail too high and that's why it happened to me the first time. As an adult, I told myself for a while that it was my fault because I was weak, too friendly, too ambitious. At times I felt I was really only good for one thing. I don't truly believe that but the experiences I had certainly made me second guess myself again.

Meanwhile, some believe it's okay to treat women as objects rather than valued respected colleagues. I'm glad the #MeToo movement came to be, but our society still has a way to go in making sure women, girls and two-spirited people are safe even in the workplace. Again, of course men and boys too. No one should ever feel degraded at work or in their life. I believe the issue has yet to be fully addressed in Indigenous communities, but it is happening in some ways. I also believe there are more men who work hard every day to show women, girls and two-spirited people the respect we deserve. These men outnumber the men who don't. There is hope, and it's to the credit of strong people who stand up against sexism and all forms of violence.

Who should be speaking up though? Men, women, or both? Other women, women in power and those struggling to survive, who've experienced the same thing also say they don't and won't speak up because they don't want to be blacklisted in any way either. I think when you've been shut out for so long and you work hard to get where you are, you sometimes tolerate things like misogyny and chauvinism to maintain what you've managed to achieve. Not all people of course, because some find a way to speak out. But sadly, speaking out against sexism and abuse of any kind in Indigenous communities is still rare. I think there's also a fear of not being believed, stemming again from colonization, the Indian Residential School System and Sixties Scoop eras for example, that taught many of our people to stay quiet about bad incidents we experience. Still, I think the Indigenous #MeToo movement hasn't reached its peak just yet. I think it will take strong and brave leaders to bring this out in the open and therefore create safer spaces within Indigenous circles as well.

Chapter 26

MKO

I was the MKO Grand Chief for one term, three years, and I was fortunate enough to work with brilliant people, including all the Chiefs who I was answerable to. We got a lot done in a short amount of time. Sometimes it felt like we weren't getting anywhere, but in actuality we accomplished much. For one, from the first day in office we worked to strengthen our people's role as the caregivers of our children in care by regaining control over the governing body of the child welfare agencies that existed in our territories. It took us almost the whole three years to get it done, partly because the provincial government officials of the day kept changing the markers when we achieved the hurdles they put in front of us. It wasn't until the government changed hands that we were able to regain the control of the Northern Authority of Manitoba.

The Northern Authority (NA) is a Manitoba provincial organization that oversees the work of individual child welfare offices throughout the North. Through the NA the Province of Manitoba has ultimate control over the children in care. Before I became the MKO GC, incidents happened where the province felt they had to take supreme authority over the NA away from MKO, where chiefs and organizations officials were the ones who did the actual work to oversee the Child and Family Service agencies. The province accused MKO of political interference and took control of NA by installing its own board that didn't include Chiefs or MKO. The Chiefs wanted the authority back and we worked on the issue almost daily until the new provincial PC government in 2017 allowed it to happen.

We also managed to strengthen the financial oversight of the organization. The former Grand Chief's tenure was marred with allegations of mismanagement but very quickly, thanks to the Chief and Councillors I worked with, we drew up and imposed stronger measures in spending. The long-serving staff told me the morale and integrity of the organization had taken a big hit and, in our time together we managed to build it back up quickly. Again, we were able to achieve that with the support of the leaders I worked with. I was also able to have a multimillion-dollar debt built up by the previous administration cleared before I left office.

In the three years I was the MKO Grand Chief, our office was also able to increase national and international awareness about MMIW. As an organization and as an advocate of MMIW myself, we became one of the 'go to' voices in the media on the topic. This was certainly a role we couldn't and didn't take lightly. We worked hard to make sure families, survivors, and others affected by MMIW were represented well by all of us at MKO. To help with that we secured funds to hire someone who could concentrate on this issue. The decision to do so was unanimously supported by our Chiefs and Councillors.

But the biggest achievement perhaps, was our relentless effort to convince the federal government to work with us and let us from northern Manitoba create, operate, and run our own health entity. The idea was ignited after a forum our organization had on health just a few months into my mandate. One of the Chiefs expressed his frustration within six months of my leadership about the government's reluctance to commit more resources for the health of his people. The other Chiefs agreed and wanted to host a rally highlighting their frustrations. I felt those frustrations and I wanted to act on them, but I had to take a break right at that time to tend to a health matter myself. So, the work to get our own health entity had to wait a few weeks.

I took a quick break because I was offered a full hip replacement surgery by my orthopedic doctor. I took the offer because we weren't sure when the surgery would be available to me again. The pain in my hips was worse than ever and getting more painful every day. Walking even just a half hour created a lot of pain but it was there even when I was sitting. The pain would sometimes wake me up at night too. It wasn't unusual for me to take painkillers all day long. So, I gladly, but a little reluctantly, took the offer for the hip replacement. I told the Chief at the health assembly we were at, "I won the lottery." It got their attention, but they laughed with me when I said it was the health lottery.

The plan was to do the other hip a year after that. Both hips were replaced a year apart, the first on my birthday in April, the second one a day after my birthday the following year. The moment I was conscious enough from the first surgery, I felt a tremendous difference in my hip. It felt solid and pain-free. Even though the surgery was only about two hours before, I was up and walking some. I was up and walking on the same day as my surgeries for both hips, and again I instantly felt stronger. I could not believe what a difference the new hips made as I walked, it was like a night and day difference. I was up and about a week after each of the surgeries, attending and speaking at events. It took about six weeks to fully heal and walk without crutches, but even recovering from the surgeries was less painful than having my original hips that had been somewhat repaired twenty plus years before my replacements.

While recovering from the surgeries, I worked with Jennifer, Darcy, and the fabulous Shaun Loney on a Ten-Point Economic Action Plan. While I was convalescing at home, I talked with all three of them about ideas on how we could tackle some of the issues I was learning about at MKO. Darcy and his colleague, Shaun, worked together on social enterprise initiatives. This was work that I loved and had trained for back in Brandon when I first got into college in 1994. When we first started talking about it, we were discussing practical solutions to things such as unemployment, underemployment, food insecurity, and high cost of living on reserves. We brainstormed and came up with ten ideas that could be easily implemented by governments and communities, should they choose to.

In the plan, for example, was an idea that was already being implemented in St. Theresa Point, Manitoba—a car crushing plant where cars were recycled after useful parts had been removed. The idea was to expand the work to all northern First Nations because each community has hundreds of broken-down vehicles. The vehicles are left there because of a lack of garages or mechanics to fix them when they break down, which creates an eyesore and potentially an environmental threat to the local area.

Another idea was to take an inventory of available jobs on reserve and doing a study that could look at what's needed to fill the jobs and match education and resources to needs. The whole ten-point plan was to get people thinking about what they could do to improve their lives and work toward a greater sense of self-sufficiency.

The plan was also a call to action for the federal, provincial, and municipal governments by giving them ideas on what they could support on First Nations reserves. The plan caught the attention of researchers at Brandon University who suggested they do a study on the economic contributions that Indigenous people made to the province annually. My office and I helped to secure some funds to get the study done and we provided someone from my office to participate in the work, the late Clyde Flett, who also worked on my MKO campaign in 2015. He sadly passed away from Covid-19 in December 2020. Clyde was an excellent researcher and assistant. And he was a valued member of my original MKO campaign team and loved dearly by his family and friends.

The study by Brandon University was released after I was done my term, but what the study found was that Indigenous People contributed $9.3 billion a year to the Manitoba economy. Proving what many of us knew already, Indigenous People, businesses, and organizations are contributing partners of the province, while still suffering the effects of shortsighted and even racist government policies, legislations by all levels of government that contribute to the poverty and misery of Indigenous People.

The plan itself did get a lot of people from the different levels of government looking at it, commenting on it and wondering how they could make it work. But the only point that was truly implemented was a drivers' licensing program for First Nations on reserves. Our argument was that if we don't get people to study for and get driver's licenses then they'll have a hard time even applying for a job. The Manitoba government agreed and implemented a new program that has helped hundreds of First Nations get their DL's, which of course became a valuable piece of identification as well. Many First Nations struggle with getting ID they need, especially on reserves.

On the health front, after my first surgery I started working with our own MKO researchers to make an argument to the governments to let our people have their own health entity. On reserves, both the federal and provincial governments are involved in delivering health programs for Indigenous people, though the provinces were given the authority by the federal government to administer health services in their respective provinces. This was originally done through the Natural Resources Transfer Agreement. In this arrangement, First Nations health was never fully resourced, and it seems the situation gets worse every year. Much like any program on reserves, governments deliver the bare minimum of what's actually needed. And when there are disputes on whether the provincial or federal governments should pay for health care, people get sicker or even die while they are waiting.

This was the sad case of Jordan River Anderson of Norway House, Manitoba. He was born with special needs but instead of getting what he needed on reserve, he died in the hospital before the Province of Manitoba and Government of Canada stopped going back and forth on who should pay the medical expenses for the boy to be closer to home. Another huge movement started after he died, and eventually Jordan's Principle was struck and passed, saying in essence that any child on any First Nation with special needs who requires any type of medical care or resource should get it. This is one of the arguments we sadly had to point out when we talked to the then Federal Health Minister, Jane Philpott.

To make the case even stronger, our MKO health researchers, led by Inez Vystrcil-Spence, pulled together the thirty years of Chiefs' resolutions to show what they've been wanting to see in terms of improving health outcomes on reserves. Inez and her team pulled together unfulfilled mandates, called resolutions, passed by MKO Chiefs in assemblies over the past thirty years to see what the commonalities between them were. The calls for health transformation were one of the main findings in the study and we began working to craft an argument that would allow us to create and manage our own northern First Nations health entity.

We began teaming up with a sister organization from northern Ontario, Nishinabe Aski Nation, where my friend Alvin Fiddler was the Grand Chief, and Dr. Alika Lafontaine the President of the Canadian Medical Association in 2021. We worked together with other specialists to create the plans for health entities in our respective regions. We wanted the entities to be designed by, and run by and for Indigenous people because we saw it as the only way they would succeed given the fact that governments did such a poor job in delivery thus far. We knew this to be true based on discouraging health statistics we pulled together of our regions that showed First Nations in our areas were among the sickest in the whole country. High rates of diabetes, cancers, tuberculosis, suicides, and high mortality rates, for example. We wanted to see different outcomes, better outcomes for our people

With the information and knowledge in hand I maximized every opportunity I had to tell federal ministers Philpott and ISC's Carolyn Bennett that we needed to make the northern Manitoba Indigenous health entity a reality. I would talk to either of them when I saw them, even when I would run into them at an airport. And we didn't just wait for them to act. Our office started creating the framework for such an entity. We had the statistics, the calls for action from Chiefs and Councils going back again to the beginning of MKO and we identified the capacity needed to build the framework.

When I was done my term in 2018, the beginnings of an agreement we worked hard to get were finally in place. Nearly 50 million dollars was committed to support the creation of the northern Manitoba Indigenous health entity and the work began just before the Covid pandemic hit the world. While the health entity was still in development when the virus made its devastating appearance in northern Manitoba, the need to have it became clearer than ever.

One of the coolest things that happened while we were working toward health transformation with Grand Chief Fiddler was getting to meet Gord Downie! Just before my first general assembly as the new MKO Grand Chief, The Tragically Hip had finished their final cross-Canada tour. In the last concert, which was broadcast live on the CBC network, Gord Downie tried to inspire other Canadians to do better for Indigenous people, saying Prime Minister Justin Trudeau was the PM that could get the work done to improve lives of Indigenous people. He said, "We're in good hands, folks, real good hands. He (PM Trudeau) cares about the people way up North, that we were trained our entire lives to ignore, trained our entire lives to hear not a word of what's going on up there. And what's going on up there ain't good. It's maybe worse than it's ever been. (But) we're going to get it fixed and we got the guy to do it, to start, to help," Gord said passionately.

I didn't see the show at first, but I recorded it. The night he made those statements though, many people from across Canada were asking me if I saw Gord saying that. I hadn't but I watched it as soon as I could the next morning. I wasn't expecting to be impacted by his statements the way I was. Hearing them, seeing his heart pour out like that hit me like a ton of bricks. I sat there crying happy tears. I felt like he was actually standing next to us as Chiefs and Leaders who stood and stand every day holding up their people as best we could. At that moment I felt like he was helping us with the heavy lifting.

All I could do was post on Twitter. I said, "#GordDownie needs to know we appreciate his care/concern 4 Indigenous ppl @perrybellegarde @gcfiddler @Tony_Alexis @ChiefDay @makwa_d et al at 9:30 am on August 21st, 2016.

I was hoping that anyone who knew him, any fellow Grand Chiefs, who could personally talk to him or see him, would thank him for me and all Indigenous people in Manitoba. Not long after that, media started calling me, asking why I posted that. Then my friend Alvin Fiddler called and asked if I wanted to thank him myself. I said, "Yes, of course." Later that week after my spring MKO Chiefs Assembly, I joined Alvin, Gord, and his two brothers, Mike and Patrick, Stuart Coxe, and a film crew in Thunder Bay, Ontario.

Documentary producers and friends Mike Downie and Stuart Coxe were working on telling the story of Chanie Wenjack before Gord got involved in creating the music for it and bringing world-wide attention to it. Mike and Stuart were already on the verge of making the story well-known but as soon as Gord heard about it, he wanted to help. Chanie was a student/prisoner at the Cecilia Jeffrey Indian Residential School in Kenora, Ontario when he escaped and tried to run home, following a railroad track toward his home community and family at Ogoki Post (Martin Falls) in northern Ontario. He died before he could reach home 600 kilometers away. His frozen body was found on the tracks a week after he ran away.

Gord and his band had just finished their cross-Canada tour as a farewell tour to thank his fans for all of their support and love for them. Gord was diagnosed with cancer; he had a brain tumor. He felt compelled to spend the last days of his life helping others and chose to help Indigenous people get the attention they needed for a better life. He heard of Chanie and asked to help Mike and Stuart tell the story. To do that, he wanted to meet Chanie's family, and the plan was for all of them to take a trip to his community after the cross-Canada Tragically Hip tour was done. They needed area Chiefs to help them organize the visit, and that's where Grand Chief Alvin Fiddler came in, and how I came to be invited on such a rare and beautiful opportunity.

We had supper the first night I flew out to meet everyone in Thunder Bay, to talk about our trip to visit Ogoki Post in Marten Falls reserve in northern Ontario. Gord wanted to meet the family of Chanie Wenjack and see where the boy who died running away from a residential school was from. We spent time with the family, watched the film crew gathering special moments with Gord and the Wenjack family, and ate with other community members.

The first time I met Gord, we were both wearing jean jackets. He walked up to me and said, "nice jacket." I told him I liked his too. From that moment on I witnessed Gord's tender heart and the love he had for everyone around him. He was quiet at times and super energetic other times. I certainly saw the vulnerable side of him, at times he seemed very lonely and lethargic. One time he whispered to me that he was cold while we were at a community feast. I told him that he was getting a blanket shortly in a Blanketing Ceremony and that would warm him up. I wish I had the blanket for him sooner though, he was shivering. Shortly, GC Alvin and his staff got up to present him with the blanket, wrapping it around him to signify their appreciation and love for him. He loved it.

He also took time to drum with the drum group that came on the trip; he was very subdued as everyone surrounded the drum circle. I snapped pictures of course, and in one picture it's almost like there was a face of a white bear over top of his face, like a mask. I showed it to him, and he choked back a little and thanked me.

In one of the quiet times during the filming of *Secret Path* at Ogoki Post, he asked me about my kids. He asked, "Are they good kids?" I said, "Yes." He said, "Oh good, good." I felt he genuinely wanted to know. From there and before he passed, we exchanged several texts and phone calls. He was always generous with his time, his love, and expressing his compassion for Indigenous people. He asked me about my kids and also talked about his own kids and family, he was so proud of them.

I was at the AFN assembly in Ottawa when Gord was given his spiritual name, "Man who walks among the Stars." I was invited to join the stage with Gord, GC Alvin, Prime Minister Justin Trudeau, AFN National Chief Bellegarde and others. When it was done, he hugged everyone and came over to hug me as he cried on my shoulder and whispered, "This is the greatest day of my life." Gord was a beautiful man, with a beautiful heart. He died three days after my father died in October 2017. I got the news as my family and I boarded a plane to take my dad home to Bunibonibee. I imagined they got to meet each other in heaven, the idea was bittersweet and made me happy.

There were many special moments in the three years I was the Grand Chief of MKO, attending graduations and honouring ceremonies among them. There were some hard times as well, such as having to have very serious discussions with people in positions of power. One particular discussion stands out in my mind. I had to talk to a former Winnipeg Police Chief (not Danny Smyth) about racism in our city and among the ranks of WPS including one spokesperson who berated me several times while I was still reporting just a year before. He didn't take it too kindly to hear what I had to say, and neither did I when he kept making condescending statements to me while we discussed the issue in my office. All the while I was thinking, if I'm having a hard time talking to the police about concerns I see, how are our relatives able to make their voices heard. Even the police chief was being dismissive and disrespectful to me as a Grand Chief. Jennifer Wood was my special assistant at the time, and she recalls that conversation as being 'very tough' and that it made her want to crawl under the table! It might have been when the police chief kept talking about how my 'feelings' were hurt in a condescending way. He also threatened to go to the media about the facts of our conversation.

I took exception to that and finally told him to go ahead with the facts he had about our conversation. I said, "You have your facts, so do I. And I also have feelings (in the long-drawn condescending way he said the word), and I will make them known" I said. In the end we got through the conversation, but it definitely was awkward. The same police chief resigned weeks after our conversation, for reasons only he would know.

I was the face of MKO, but I certainly don't feel like I did any of the things we did alone. I am extremely grateful to the smart and capable people I worked with, including Jennifer and Inez Vystrcil-Spence. Her research and writing skills are superb, her ability to find the right people for the work we needed to do was exceptional. I also worked with others in the organization, including the executive director Kelvin Lynxleg, who had reputations of being some of the hardest and kindest workers people have come across. Not a surprise to me or anyone who's ever lived in the North though. It's part of our people's nature and abilities. Of course, Jennifer Wood was with me the whole time and despite her battle with cancer during our work with MKO, she finished the work with me. She too had an amazing ability to find and recruit other people we needed to get work done. I loved my time at MKO and it was an honour to see our organization gain national and international attention for our work.

Chapter 27

SYSTEMIC RACISM

Experiencing racism is like a gut punch. It can ruin your entire day and make you feel sick. It does for me, like food poisoning or coming off a carnival ride that makes you dizzy. And I can recall almost every time I ever faced racism and racists. One of the first clear memories of it was as a teenager new to Winnipeg. I walked into a little convenience store and there were two young guys saying something and laughing at me. I had no idea what they said but I remember feeling so bad about myself, I felt worthless. Another time, my little brother and sisters were crossing a street during one of our family trips to Winnipeg. We were all so excited to be in the city and when my brother saw a nice car in front of us, he tapped it lightly on the hood. The driver, a grown man, jumped out and told my little brother, who was about ten years old, to "Get your hands of my fucking car, you dirty Indian," right in the middle of traffic on the street. We all felt so bad for him, I felt ill.

As we got older and started going to post-secondary school, one of my sisters was looking for an apartment. We were so excited to see a place and the landlord set up a time for her to stop in to see it. We hopped on the bus and got there. We knocked. We waited. We knocked some more and realized the landlord took one look at us from inside and chose not to let us in! I felt so horrible for my excited sister. It wasn't a good feeling. We knew it wasn't because he was busy, he took one look at us and decided not to even talk to us.

But one of the worst moments I've experienced racism is when I was a young mom in Brandon. I used to take my kids riding on their little tricycles in our neighbourhood all the time. One day we went out a little further than our normal route. As we passed by this one house, I saw a man standing in his doorway staring at me and my kids. I knew he was fixated on us because he stood there, holding a mug not saying anything. I tried to get the kids past the house quickly and I thought we were safe after we passed his house. But as we turned a corner on the sidewalk, my little girl ran over a corner of his lawn with her little red tricycle. That was enough to trigger the man in the doorway. He threw down his mug, yelled, and came running towards us onto the sidewalk. He shouted, "Get your fucking bike of my fucking property you dirty Indians." I was horrified and my kids were nervous. I didn't say anything back to the man, I just quickly got my kids home.

My ex-husband was still living with us at the time, and I told him what happened. He was so angry and made me show him where the man lived. I was hesitant to tell him because I know how he got when he was angry. But calmly he told me he just wanted to talk to the guy, so reluctantly I took him to the house. He knocked and when the man opened the door and saw my ex-husband and me in the background, I knew he knew what the visit was about. My ex said, "Can you come out here? I want to talk about what happened with my kids and my wife." He asked him to come out, that he just wanted to talk to him. The man refused at first but eventually he did. My ex is convincing. As soon as he stepped on the sidewalk, my ex punched him in the face over and over again, asking him, "What is it like to be punched out by an Indian?"

They were full-on fighting when a woman behind me started yelling for them to stop. They eventually did and we went home. Police were not far behind and came to talk to us about the incident. In the end no charges were laid because police said they were both fighting! But what an ordeal that was. It not only hurt, but it also angered me that my precious innocent children were subjected to such hatred. I wished my ex hadn't lost his temper and fought with the guy, but he was fiercely protective of our children. That was the worst display of racism I had ever felt.

As I grew older and began to work away from home, I started to feel more confident about myself as a Cree person. I started realizing that the racism and racist attitudes directed at me were more about the other person than me. So, it got easier to deal with and it no longer ruined my whole day. But that didn't stop it from happening over and over again.

One of the last times I felt overt racism was while I was still a Grand Chief. I was getting ready for New Year's Eve. After a workout, I needed to go to a pharmacy for a couple of things, so I ran in quickly in my workout clothes. It is normal for me to feel followed and watched by store security guards in many places I shop at. Most of the time I've learned to ignore the guards watching or following me. But this one time, as I heard an intercom announcement summoning security to a certain section of the pharmacy, I was hoping the aisle being called out wasn't the one I was standing alone in. I looked up to check and sure enough there I was, in aisle five where security was being called to!

I sighed and was going to keep shopping but I remembered what my sweet mom had told me just a few days before. After security guards followed her around as she shopped, she said she felt bad and worthless. I didn't like hearing that and I thought, if we don't speak out against this kind of discrimination it will keep happening. I grabbed a few more things and headed to the checkout to ask the young clerk why she called security to where I was. She denied it and said it was random. Maybe so, but I still needed to say something to them all because they acted like what I was saying and feeling wasn't important. The store manager eventually came out and apologized for the incident.

I posted a story about the incident on social media and I ended up doing several media interviews about the racist incident. I took the opportunity to tell anyone who experienced or witnessed racism to speak up and say something when it happens to them. I see speaking out against racism every time anyone encounters it as the only way to eventually put an end to it.

But hidden racism is probably one of the worst forms of racism, when you know someone is treating you a certain way because of who you are. Or who you are as a people. It usually comes out as patronizing behaviour and it seems people in positions of power are the ones who use this form the most, people who have the authority to make decisions over others. The federal government with its Indian Act is a prime example. It reinforces racist attitudes toward Indigenous people and gives life to systemic racism.

Systemic racism is ingrained in everything and every aspect of our lives. It's almost as normal as breathing but in a life deprecating way! And what I've come to understand and believe is that we all as a country have grown up to accept systemic racism by treating Indigenous people with disdain and hatred our whole lives. And as we did, people took that mindset with them into their lives as police officers, doctors, lawyers, grocery store clerks, politicians, and our neighbours! Many of us as Indigenous people learned to accept some of it because we don't always see ourselves as people to be treated with the same level of respect that everyone else expects for themselves.

I often wonder what life would be like for Indigenous people without racism and hate. I choose to dream about a life without it. Especially now that I'm a grandmother, a Kookom to my first grandchild, my Noosisim, Adonis. I wish to eradicate racism before Noosisim and any other future grandchildren are old enough to be impacted by it. I wish that by the time they are old enough to make decisions for themselves, our country will be where they are able to go after any dream they may have, using all of their God-given gifts and talents in any way they choose to, without hindrances and racist obstacles. And most of all, I hope they won't face situations where they have to justify who they are, where they choose to live, or how they choose to live their life. I'd like all our future generations to have the same opportunities. It's important for my family and yours, Indigenous and non-Indigenous.

I consider myself an eternal optimist and I choose to remain hopeful about ending racism, which I think is just as bad if not worse than the global pandemic we are all living through. It will take all of us to influence lasting changes. But to create lasting positive changes we need to be bold as a country so we may influence those in power to change laws and policies that harm or limit people, like the Indian Act. Or we can wait and hope for people in power to do it on their own. From what I witnessed in the MMIW movement, Idle No More, Rock the Vote, seeing what happened during the Black Lives Matter rallies, and the Civil Rights Movement for example it's the people who make the difference. We the people have to be the ones to initiate lasting positive changes for our societies. Even if 'we' means politicians as well.

Chapter 28

MY RUN FOR AFN

In 2018 decided to run as a candidate to become the National Chief of the Assembly of First Nations after being approached by Chiefs in several provinces to run. It was a long shot and I had lost my dad just a few months before I decided to run. I think his passing made me fearless, fearless of death anyway. I thought what could be worse than losing the strongest person I knew. So, running and going against my own fears was something I was able to do for the greater good. I also wanted to make my late father proud, and I thought it would encourage my mom, my kids, and the rest of my family to see something good happening in our lives. But I also wanted the best for our people, and I wanted to be part of making life better for all of us, and when the opportunity came knocking to run, I answered the call.

When we got going in the campaign, I was kept busy and my campaign team and I travelled throughout the country to try and meet the over six hundred Chiefs, who are the only ones who are allowed to vote in the AFN election. Some seek to change that, to include votes from all First Nations people. I think that could and should happen someday so Grand Chiefs and National Chiefs can truly say that they represent the people in their territory or region. I met with many Chiefs, Councillors, and Community Leaders to gather their ideas, and I shared some of those ideas in my final speech. Learning about the issues was one of the memories I will cherish the most about the election.

The election to become the National Chief was a short but a mighty one. Most elections for Chiefs, Grand Chiefs, and National Chiefs are short, just a few weeks. This one was mighty for many good and bad reasons. The AFN election was good in itself because I was able to meet many more incredible people from across the country. I learned so much about the richness of our beautiful and strong Nations. I saw and felt the hope and optimism in the faces of our people in spite of all the challenges they and their families have been through. I saw the displays of culture and heard people speaking ancient languages that I will never forget. I got to see and feel the vastness of our lands, water, and air. We truly live in one of the best places in the world.

On the wrong side, I saw and felt things that I know stems from colonization, such as lateral violence where some people tear each other down in order to get what they need, no matter the cost. For Indigenous people, I realize there are many things that cause people to act the way they do, including being misogynistic or ignorant. Indigenous peoples have been forced to absorb the racism they're subjected to and came to believe that they are lesser people. That causes some to lash out against each other. What hurt the most was seeing and hearing adults, respected adults, who've also come through so much in life, act like bullies I've come across my whole life.

One particular moment that's been seared in my mind was when several adult males who could be considered Elders from one of the other AFN campaign teams surrounded me and yelled directly into my ear to, "Back off. Concede." I was shocked. The incident momentarily took me back to Bunibonibee when I was a small child, being surrounded by the swarm of dogs who could've easily ripped me apart. The barks and harsh comments from this group of grown men surrounding me sounded very familiar. But I didn't have a kind one in the circle to help me at that moment.

Another example was when a fellow candidate openly made fun of me by making jokes about my age, even suggesting one time that I was still wearing diapers. I felt attacked several times during the campaign, especially near the end of the race. Not physically, but spiritually. I've only experienced a spiritual attack once before, though I'm sure it has happened during other times as well. You feel more than you see spiritual attacks, but they have the ability to make you feel sick, scared and even mentally unstable. Worse than the feeling of a gut punch when you experience racism, and worse than the lack of confidence you feel when someone unleashes lateral violence on you. The spiritual attacks are ones you can only explain in person. I only tell a few people about those incidents because I feel I can and should only share the true facts of what I felt with other praying people. I've been able to overcome the pain from attacks and I don't want to give the attacks or attackers any more of my time and power.

Admittedly, I didn't feel I was qualified to run for AFN during that time. I felt inadequate and not prepared. But that was the same feeling I had had when I ran for MKO three years prior. However, I learn fast, and I was confident that I'd be able to get a good team around me to help me fulfill my duties, as I had at MKO.

Thankfully and intentionally, I managed to run a clean campaign that didn't run a deficit. I felt accomplished that we came in second when it was all said and done. But the lateral violence some in other campaigns displayed was deplorable. Inherently it was a competition, I get that. And it's politics, yes, but I still think politics can be done respectfully. I don't believe the current way we as Indigenous people run elections is necessarily the right way. It doesn't match the love and respect our ancestors taught us to have and display, as they did during Treaty-making time. And certainly not the way Indigenous Governments, women, used to appoint Leaders the way they did before colonization. When you listen to Elders talk about appointing or grooming leaders, Treaty-making time, or welcoming settlers into our lands, we treated everyone with compassion and truly considered the best interest of everyone, not just ourselves. Now, Indigenous elections resemble non-Indigenous systems where it seems it's all about competition and a fight, winning at all costs.

However, I don't take any of the experiences for granted or give myself credit for any of it. I'm grateful for all of it. Truthfully, I was able to do the work as MKO Grand Chief and as a candidate to become the AFN National Chief in July of 2018 and in July 2021 for the AMC Grand Chief role because I prayed and trusted others who worked with me. I also know my parents and others prayed along with me. But the run for AFN nearly killed me—literally and figuratively! Literally because I got very sick during the AFN campaign. I developed pneumonia that persisted for many weeks even after taking antibiotics for it. I was very sick; I lost my voice and my energy. Spiritually, a healer told me the physical pains were a result of the attacks my opponents had placed on me. I have never believed in any of that, until I experienced it myself.

In spite of all that, most of the people I met were amazing and supportive, even ones who said they wouldn't vote for me. All of the places I visited were welcoming and listened to what I had to say. And I'll forever appreciate all of the Chiefs and People who supported my team's genuine efforts to make a positive influence in our country.

As for the AMC election, it severely and negatively impacted my belief in some of our people. Running in this election was truly an honour and I feel blessed I was asked to run and supported by respected Elders and long serving Chiefs of Manitoba, including David Crate, Christian Sinclair, Richard Hart, Nelson Moody, Glenn Hudson, Cornell McLean, John Stagg, Orville Smoke, Derrick Henderson, and Eric Redhead.

I had an amazing campaign team, led of course by Jennifer and Darcy Wood. On our team we had my friend Inez Vystrcil-Spence; a former Winnipeg police officer, Susan Swan; business leaders Nick Chief and Barbara Bowes; my children Trisha and Sonny; as well as Chelsea and Cory Fiddler. We were small but mighty. We got a lot done with several good partners and everything was looking good to see me elected. But sadly, for me and for the Chiefs and people who supported me, the misogyny and chauvinism, in my humble opinion, made way again for someone else to win. I was penalized for calling out sexist views that I felt were detrimental to our people. Some men and women took that opportunity to paint me as an angry bitter woman who would use the sexist card whenever it suited me. Nothing could've been further from the truth. I wanted and still want the best for our people. And one of the Chiefs who tried to intimidate me by saying he had so much influence during the MKO election was there again, acting like he was a victim of my words when I called out his sexism. But it is what it is. I've accepted that loss and have moved on.

Though I will say, again, I have received support since the election from many people who were hoping I would win, including young women and men who told me I had a strong heart. And that they hope to run in elections some day. I hope so too, and I hope the world will be ready for them too.

During my run in both of the AFN and AMC elections I learned first-hand how we as Indigenous people in this country are diverse and unique. While there are many similarities and we have shared experiences, the opinions about life and philosophy are as different as the regions we all come from. All of those differences are valid of course, and our varying views need to be respected if we expect to see successful self-sufficient Indigenous people. Many from our Nations will say we are already successful and self-sufficient. That we don't need other governments to make that happen for those Nations that aren't. I agree, but I also believe that because of colonization our communities and families have been disrupted from living the life we once had as independent sovereign nations before colonization.

I believe we need to get to a place where more Indigenous people, including women, girls, two-spirited people, young people, and people living with other challenges including health and mental health ones, feel included and empowered. Not feeling less than or not deserving of basic human rights that many in our rich country take for granted. Let's never forget that the Original People of these lands and all their descendants, me, Noosisim, my kids, my family, and any Indigenous person you know, are subjected to third world conditions in our own lands. None of us should be alright with that, and I hope we all work together to end the hate, discrimination, and racism toward Indigenous people in Canada. How? By calling out all these negative stereotypes every time we witness them and use every opportunity we have to speak up and say something. I love allies too. My friend Mary Scott from Winnipeg is one of the best ones I've seen. She, with her beautiful heart and white privilege, opens doors for others to walk in, and she does it so gracefully. Mary has done this for me and many others over the years; she did it for me by inviting me to the United Nations in New York twice to talk about MMIW.

Through all the people I've met in my life and all the experiences I've had, I've learned we need to get back to a place where we as Indigenous people run our own affairs. Governments built on systemic racism have never honoured and respected the historic Treaties and Agreements signed by our people and the British Crown, and they cannot be trusted to have our best interests in mind. Treaties and Agreements signed since colonization were meant to establish good relationships between Indigenous people and new Canadians. We were intended to become partners and to live peaceably with each other in the vast and resource-rich country now known as Canada. The time to honour those Treaties and Agreements is long overdue, and I believe our people are now pushing harder than ever to see that our people are not ignored, disrespected or forgotten anymore. I hope to see another level of government in my lifetime, one where Indigenous People govern themselves and our people, our lands, complete with the appropriate resources needed to promote and protect all Original People of this country now known as Canada. I continue to support the work that moves toward that vision.

Chapter 29

TODAY, TOMORROW, THE FUTURE

As I got busier in my role as an elected leader, my personal life started to change dramatically too. Rob and I started to do better financially as a couple, but our family drifted apart. The man who brought me closer to my children when I was struggling to be a good mother after my separation with my ex-husband was getting busy too. In the meantime, I was working as the MKO Grand Chief, working with my film partner to get the MMIW film done, and recovering from my hip surgeries. I was out of town a lot, much like he was during our seventeen-year marriage while he was performing at shows or speaking at events throughout Canada and the US.

Unfortunately, we separated in the second year of my term as Grand Chief and we ultimately divorced when I was done. It was really tough; I didn't want our marriage to end but I also didn't have or make time to save it. We are still respectful of each other, and I will always love him and cherish the time we had together. I feel the same about my first ex-husband, lovely man (sarcasm is sometimes the best way I can approach difficult topics). But I truly don't hold any bitterness against him. He acted the way he did because of the sad reality of his childhood, largely connected to what happened to many of our people during the beginning of the colonization process. I will forever love him. I hope someday he will be able to see his kids again and meet our beautiful grandson.

I don't consider my life just a privilege anymore; rather, I consider it a responsibility to live my best life. No matter what it has in store and what I've experienced so far. A very smart man who studied politics for most of his life told me before he passed that if people are asking me to run for office, I have to listen to the people. To give them what they want. While I don't always feel adequate to lead, I do feel the immense need to help where and when I can.

Many influencers on the internet who teach others how to be successful say we have to make decisions that are best for us as individuals. But that's not how I was taught. I saw my parents emptying their fridge several times to help feed other families who came to our doors looking for help. I saw them give anything they had to help anyone in need and so did my community, my people. That is the kind of world I want to live in, where we all help each other in times of need.

My mom and late dad chose to help others the way they did and chose to raise us the way they did because they are inherently good people. Much like all of our Indigenous ancestors. While they drew from the teachings from the Bible (Loving God, Love Your Neighbour, Forgive, Love Your Enemies, Ask God for Forgiveness, Jesus is the Messiah, Repentance of Sin is essential), the teachings they taught us have many similarities to the Seven Teachings many Indigenous people adhere to (Love, Respect, Courage, Honesty, Wisdom, Humility, Truth). I know my mom and dad and other spiritual teachers I've met embodied what's good about Our God, Our Creator and I'm very grateful they all taught me the same, and I try to teach my future generations the same.

However, I never assume or act like I'm perfect in any way. I know my flaws. I still struggle with asserting myself, I still struggle with my self-esteem, and I still struggle to find what true love is.

Life is hard and I applaud anyone who never gives up. I try to live that way as well. But while I applaud anyone who achieves or teaches about individual success, I think as Indigenous people we see success differently. When our people are healthy and our families have what they need, that's success. Now that I'm a proud kookom, I see the importance of that even more. While I was a young parent, I struggled many times, and it seemed I was always in survival mode. Sometimes I feel bad that I had my amazing children at such a young age and that I dragged them through a life that was sometimes hard for us. Sometimes I wish I could start all over and raise my children differently, but I suppose all parents feel that way every now and then. One thing I do know is my children are strong, strong-hearted, and beautiful human beings. They've been my greatest motivators and being their mother and now being a kookom is the greatest honour I've been gifted with. In fact, of all the amazing opportunities I've been given and have taken in my life, being a mother and kookom are my favourite roles so far. I feel blessed and my mind is always on what I can do to make life better, easier, and nicer for them. Which also makes me love my parents and siblings and extended family even more, because I realize that they too probably feel the same way.

And even though life as a young mom was not always easy, I learned to find a way to get what I needed for my children and myself. Now for my Noosisim (and even my fur grand-dog Doug) I have a longer view and am committed to making life better for him and our future generations.

I imagine that our ancestors who worked on negotiating and signing the Treaties or made Agreements with governments had a long view as well. They would have had to, because the Treaties and Agreements they signed off on address the needs of that day and those of today. Realizing this and seeing my Noosisim's little face is beyond amazing, and I see his life as a higher calling for me, for all of us, to do better. I want to keep answering the calls to do better. I hope we all do, because it's not just a privilege to be where I am, where we are in life now, it's my responsibility and your responsibility to live in the best way we can for a better future for all of us. Ekosani, Kisakihitin.

Acknowledgements

Trisha, my firstborn, Sonny my second-born and Adonis, Noosisim (my grandson): you are the greatest joys of my life. My main mission since you came in to my world is making sure you feel loved, supported, and encouraged. Thank you, Donald, for coming into our lives, you are loved.

My momma Sadie, when I think of you, I feel grateful that you and Dad raised me, my sisters and brothers the way you did. Your example of how to live life, love God and ourselves is beautiful. I miss you every day Pops, I'm so glad you taught me everything you could. I'm so thankful for you both.

Audrey, Kathleen, Rachel (Shawn), Steven (Mildred), and Harry, I cherish our childhoods, your children and grandchildren, my nieces, nephews. The memories we have together are precious.

All my relatives, you are absolutely a good force in my life. All of you. Thank you Pisim for helping me to tell my dad's side of the story.

Jennifer and Darcy, your friendship, guidance and insights are so appreciated. You are God-sent.

Inez, Barbara B, Christy, Diane, Cathy, Angie, Winona, Edna, Cory, Chief Maureen, your friendship is golden to me and I would not have been able to do what I did without you.

My media family and friends, you are all part of a dream I've had since I was very young. Very appreciated.

Chiefs, Councillors, Community Leaders I worked with, I admire your strength, wisdom, and ability to keep working in the face of hardships and uncertainty.

All MMIW families, survivors, thrivers, allies, advocates, leaders and supporters. I admire all of you.

Everyone at Great Plains Publications, Mel, Rhonda, Catharina for the encouragement and invaluable guidance on this part of the journey.

Kisahkihitinaw Kuhkinow. You are all loved by me.

Of course, I need to acknowledge God, Our Creator. Where all life, love and hope come from and who sustains me.

Lastly, YOU. Ekosi, thank you for loving me, making me laugh and even making me cry. I will always be grateful for you. You know who you are.

Ekosani